Taxing Energy Use 2018

COMPANION TO THE TAXING ENERGY USE DATABASE

This work is published under the responsibility of the Secretary-General of the OECD. The opinions expressed and arguments employed herein do not necessarily reflect the official views of OECD member countries.

This document, as well as any data and any map included herein, are without prejudice to the status of or sovereignty over any territory, to the delimitation of international frontiers and boundaries and to the name of any territory, city or area.

Please cite this publication as:
OECD (2018), *Taxing Energy Use 2018: Companion to the Taxing Energy Use Database*, OECD Publishing, Paris.
http://dx.doi.org/10.1787/9789264289635-en

ISBN 978-92-64-28943-7 (print)
ISBN 978-92-64-28963-5 (PDF)

The statistical data for Israel are supplied by and under the responsibility of the relevant Israeli authorities. The use of such data by the OECD is without prejudice to the status of the Golan Heights, East Jerusalem and Israeli settlements in the West Bank under the terms of international law.

Photo credits: Cover © Keller/Fotolia.com; © ART ENS/Fotolia.com; © EpicStockMedia/Fotolia.com.

Corrigenda to OECD publications may be found on line at: *www.oecd.org/about/publishing/corrigenda.htm*.
© OECD 2018

You can copy, download or print OECD content for your own use, and you can include excerpts from OECD publications, databases and multimedia products in your own documents, presentations, blogs, websites and teaching materials, provided that suitable acknowledgement of OECD as source and copyright owner is given. All requests for public or commercial use and translation rights should be submitted to *rights@oecd.org*. Requests for permission to photocopy portions of this material for public or commercial use shall be addressed directly to the Copyright Clearance Center (CCC) at *info@copyright.com* or the Centre français d'exploitation du droit de copie (CFC) at *contact@cfcopies.com*.

Foreword

Governments around the world have joined forces to fight global warming. The Paris Agreement sets a clear goal – limiting global average temperature increases to well below 2 degrees Celsius. This requires deep cuts in carbon emissions, starting now. Carbon taxes and other specific taxes on energy use – analysed in this report – can integrate the climate and environmental costs of energy use into prices. They are indispensable components of the policies needed to fight climate change, and will help cut air pollution and other negative side effects of energy use.

Energy and carbon taxes are also a new source of revenues to help fund vital government services and foster the development of affordable and clean energy. They contribute to achieving the UN's Sustainable Development Goals on access to energy and domestic resource mobilisation, in addition to combating climate change and reducing pollution.

The data presented in this report clearly show that energy taxes are failing to attain their potential contribution to reaching economic, social and environmental policy goals. Policymakers continue to miss out on making full use of these effective instruments to reach climate goals.

OECD's *Taxing Energy Use* is a unique data source, allowing for systematic comparison of the patterns of energy taxation across 42 OECD and G20 countries, disaggregated by fuels and sectors. This report presents insights on the magnitude and coverage of existing taxes on energy use, based on the second vintage of the *Taxing Energy Use* database, which contains effective tax rates on energy use for 2015. It also allows for changes between 2012 and 2015 to be observed and analysed.

Taxes on energy use differ strongly between countries, sectors and fuels, but most are well below where they should be to reflect climate costs alone, even on the basis of a truly low-end estimate of the climate cost of emissions of EUR 30 per tCO_2. Where taxes exceed this estimate, notably in road transport, other environmental impacts and considerations related to traffic congestion suggest that while taxes may be approaching the right level in a few countries, they still remain well below optimal levels in most.

Price signals from energy taxes are also very uneven across different energy products, and they are extremely low for the most carbon-intensive fuels. Taxes on oil are relatively high, while taxes on coal are often low or zero. Given its high carbon content and large air pollution impacts, aligning taxes with environmental costs calls for comparatively high taxes on the use of coal.

Apart from some steps forward in a few countries, evidence of improved use of energy taxes to address the mounting global environmental and climate challenges is very limited. Emissions trading systems, not discussed here but in the OECD's *Effective Carbon Rates*, do little to change this picture. Similarly, the intense debate on carbon taxation has sparked action, but – despite encouraging initiatives in a number of jurisdictions – has not driven any significant change in actual tax rates. Excise taxes on energy use continue dominating price signals instead of carbon taxes.

The damages from climate change and from air pollution resulting from fossil fuel combustion can be contained. However, the longer we delay in taking action, the more expensive this becomes. Well-designed taxes on energy use are a core element of cost-effective policy, and vast improvements are urgently needed. It is key that if and when compensation for cost increases from energy taxes is deemed necessary, it is provided through targeted transfers that maintain the environmental integrity of market-based instruments, not through reduced tax rates or exemptions (that apply to all, regardless of whether they deserve them). This well-known principle should be more generally observed in policy practice.

Angel Gurría
OECD Secretary-General

Acknowledgements

This report was prepared by Johanna Arlinghaus and Kurt Van Dender, with inputs from Jonas Teusch. The country notes, available online, and the data underlying the report were prepared by Johanna Arlinghaus and Melanie Marten. Johanna Arlinghaus led on the database architecture and the updates. Carrie Tyler improved the presentation and dissemination of the work. Kurt Van Dender provided oversight. All contributors are in the OECD's Centre for Tax Policy and Administration, in the case of Jonas Teusch through a joint appointment with the Environment Directorate. Peter Vogelpoel typeset the manuscript.

The authors would like to thank the following OECD colleagues for their very insightful feedback on earlier versions of the report: Nils-Axel Braathen, David Bradbury, Luisa Dressler, and Florens Flues.

The report was discussed by the OECD's Joint Meetings of Tax and Environment Experts, and it was approved for declassification by the Committee of Fiscal Affairs and the Environment Policy Committee. The authors would like to thank in particular the delegates to the Joint Meetings and their colleagues in national government administrations for their assistance with the provision of data, as well as for their invaluable suggestions, inputs and comments received at various stages of preparing the data and the report.

Table of contents

Abbreviations 9

Executive summary 11

Chapter 1. **Taxing energy use: Introduction, scope and methodology** 13
    Structure of the energy tax profiles, methodology and data sources. 15
    Methodological refinements. 17
    References 20
    Notes. 21

Chapter 2. **Patterns of taxes on energy use and changes from 2012 to 2015**. 23
    Composition of and changes in energy use and carbon emissions from energy use. 25
    Effective tax rates – key features by fuel and by sector 27
    Effective tax rates in the road sector by country 37
    Effective tax rates in non-road sectors by country 43
    ETRs and countries' broader economic characteristics. 45
    Carbon taxes by sector and fuel 47
    Conclusion 51
    References 51
    Notes. 52

Figures

Figure 2.1   Energy use by country or country groups in 2009, 2012 and 2014. 25
Figure 2.2   Composition of CO_2 emissions from energy use by sector in different country groups, 2014, % 26
Figure 2.3   Composition of CO_2 emissions from energy use by fuel for different country groups, 2014, % 26
Figure 2.4   Effective tax rates on carbon emissions from energy use on each fuel in 2015 (biomass emissions included). 27
Figure 2.5   Proportion of carbon emissions from energy use subject to different levels of effective tax rates in the road and non-road sectors, in 2012 and 2015 (excluding taxes on electricity output, including carbon emissions from biomass) 29
Figure 2.6   Effective tax rates on energy use in the 42 OECD and G20 economies in EUR/tCO_2, 2015 (excluding taxes on electricity output, including carbon emissions from biomass). . . 31
Figure 2.7   Effective tax rates on energy use in OECD countries in EUR/tCO_2, 2015 (excluding taxes on electricity output, including carbon emissions from biomass). 32
Figure 2.8   Effective tax rates on energy use in the 22 OECD economies that are also members of the European Union in EUR/tCO_2, 2015 (excluding taxes on electricity output, including carbon emissions from biomass). 33
Figure 2.9   Effective tax rates on energy use in non-EU OECD economies in EUR/tCO_2, 2015 (excluding taxes on electricity output, including carbon emissions from biomass) 34

Figure 2.10 Effective tax rates on energy use in the seven selected OECD partner economies in EUR/tCO$_2$, 2015 (excluding taxes on electricity output, including carbon emissions from biomass). ...35

Figure 2.11 Average effective tax rates from excise taxes and specific taxes on carbon by country in the road sector, in EUR/tCO$_2$, 2015 and 2012. ...38

Figure 2.12 Percentage change in average effective tax rates in the road sector by country in local currency units, 2012-15 ...39

Figure 2.13 Effective tax rates on gasoline and diesel for road use in EUR/tCO$_2$ in 2015 ...40

Figure 2.14 Percentage change in the gap between the effective tax rate on gasoline and diesel between 2012 and 2015 ...41

Figure 2.15 Estimates of marginal external costs and of fuel excise tax, France and United Kingdom, EUR/litre of gasoline and diesel ...43

Figure 2.16 Average effective tax rates from excise taxes and specific taxes on carbon by country across the non-road sectors, in EUR/tCO$_2$, 2015 and 2012 (including carbon emissions from biomass) ...44

Figure 2.17 Percentage change in average effective tax rates in the non-road sector by country in local currency units, 2012-15 ...45

Figure 2.18 Average effective tax rates on CO$_2$ emissions from energy use and GDP per capita...46

Figure 2.19 Average effective tax rates on CO$_2$ from energy and carbon intensity of energy use ...47

Figure 2.20 Average effective tax rates on CO$_2$ from energy and energy intensity of GDP ...47

Figure 2.21 Proportion of CO$_2$ emissions from energy use subject to different levels of effective tax rates from carbon taxes (biomass emissions included). ...48

Figure 2.22 Proportion of CO$_2$ emissions from energy use subject to different levels of effective tax rates from carbon taxes in countries with a carbon tax (biomass emissions included) ...49

Tables

Table 1.1 Sector classification of energy use ...18
Table 1.2 Adjustments to carbon taxes made in sectors and fuels covered by ETS ...20
Table 2.1 Share of a countries gasoline, diesel and road sector emissions in total, %, 2014 ...36

Box

Box 2.1 What is an appropriate benchmark for taxes on energy use? ...41

Abbreviations

CO_2	Carbon Dioxide
ECR	Effective Carbon Rate
EU	European Union
ETS	Emissions Trading System
IEA	International Energy Agency
GDP	Gross Domestic Product
IPCC	Intergovernmental Panel on Climate Change
OECD	Organisation for Economic Co-operation and Development
RUC	Road User Charges
SPE	Selected Partner Economies
TEU	Taxing Energy Use

Executive summary

Many forms of energy use are associated with environmental and health damages and contribute to climate change, so the social cost of energy use frequently exceeds private cost. Taxes on energy use – carbon taxes and other specific taxes on energy use – can make energy users pay for the full costs of pollution and climate change, so reducing harmful emissions at minimal cost, while also raising revenue that can fund vital government services. These considerations may affect policy design to an extent, but this report clearly shows that energy taxes continue falling well short of their potential to improve environmental and climate outcomes.

Based on OECD's *Taxing Energy Use* database, a unique dataset to compare coverage and magnitude of specific taxes on energy use across 42 OECD and G20 economies, six sectors and five main fuel types, this report assesses the magnitude and coverage of taxes on energy use in 2015, and considers change between 2012 and 2015. Together, the 42 countries represent approximately 80% of global energy use and CO_2 emissions associated with energy use. This uniquely detailed and comprehensive database is now available for 2012 and 2015.

Permit prices in CO_2 emissions trading system change the prices of energy use and carbon emissions in a way similar to the taxes included in *Taxing Energy Use*. These prices are not included here but in OECD's *Effective Carbon Rates*. However, they do little to change the findings presented here. *Taxing Energy Use* data is a key input for Effective Carbon Rates, but remains unique in its in-depth account of tax rates, particularly the breakdown by fuels.

The main findings are as follows: taxes are strongly heterogeneous, so are poorly described by country averages; almost all taxes are too low from an environmental point of view; taxes on coal often equal zero or nearly so; taxes in road transport are much higher than taxes in other sectors, but still are too low to cover external costs in nearly all cases; taxes tend to be higher where GDP per capita is higher but there are notable exceptions to this pattern; fuel taxes increased between 2012 and 2015 in some large countries, and first steps towards removing lower tax rates on diesel compared to gasoline are taken, but apart from that there are no signs that the polluter pays principle determines the energy tax landscape more strongly in 2015 than in 2012. The following paragraphs elaborate on these findings.

Energy taxes differ strongly between countries, sectors and fuels. This is the result of a mix of policy objectives and political economy factors, and it implies that consideration of average tax rates across sectors and fuels on a country level can be very misleading.

A bird's eye view of effective tax rates per tonne of CO_2 across all countries reveals that there is hardly any change in the tax rates on emissions outside the road transport sector. Taxes continue to be poorly aligned with environmental and climate costs of energy use, across all countries.

In road transport, 97% of emissions are taxed. The share of emissions taxed above climate costs increased from 46% in 2012 to 50% in 2015, and rates exceed EUR 50 per tCO_2 for 47% of emissions in 2015, compared to 37% in 2012. However, other negative side-effects suggest that taxes are at best approaching the right level in a few countries, but remain well below them in most. These changes mainly result from fuel tax reforms in China, India and Mexico.

In the non-road sectors, which collectively account for 95% of carbon emissions from energy use, 81% of emissions are untaxed, and rates are below a truly low-end estimate of climate costs of EUR 30 per tCO_2 for 97% of emissions. Between 2012 and 2015, effective tax rates decline perceptibly in real terms in around half of the countries studied, implying small and probably unintentional steps away from the polluter pays principle. To varying degrees, this is the consequence of changes in the composition of the tax base across which rates are averaged (i.e. shifts to less taxed fuels or sectors), of exchange rate movements and of nominal rates not being adjusted for inflation.

Coal, which accounts for almost half of carbon emissions in the 42 countries, goes untaxed in many countries, and is taxed above EUR 5 per tCO_2 in just 5 of the countries studied. Taxes on oil products are relatively high for all uses – they exceed EUR 100 per tCO_2 on average across all sectors – but are particularly high in road transport, a sector which remains almost entirely dependent on oil products. Counter to what would be expected on environmental grounds, taxes on diesel for road use are lower than taxes on gasoline in all but two countries, but this pattern appears to start changing in several countries.

Rates tend to be higher in countries with higher per capita GDP, although some relatively high-income countries feature relatively low average tax rates on energy use. The carbon intensity of GDP is on average lower in countries with higher tax rates on energy use. However, energy use per capita and tax rates both tend to rise strongly with income, so that per capita CO_2 emissions still rise with income on average but less so, and sometimes reversing, as income grows.

Carbon tax coverage increased from 1 to 6% between 2012 and 2015, but rates exceed climate costs for just 0.3% of emissions overall. Transport fuel taxes consist overwhelmingly of excise taxes not named a carbon tax. The contribution of carbon taxes to total rates is larger in several – mainly European – countries outside of road transport. However, the distinction between excise taxes on energy and carbon taxes is mainly nominal, with little difference in terms of economic significance, even if salience of taxes can differ depending on their visibility and name.

In sum, apart from transport fuel tax increases in some large low to middle income economies, and some first steps towards aligning diesel taxes with gasoline taxes, there is no structural change to the pattern of taxes on energy use between 2012 and 2015. This is disconcerting, particularly because improving the environment and climate effectiveness of taxes on energy use is fully compatible with more effective pursuit of the other policy objectives that have shaped current taxation patterns. If and when compensation for higher energy costs is deemed necessary, lower tax rates or exemptions are not the way to provide it – targeted transfers, that maintain the environmental integrity of market-based instruments, are superior by far.

Chapter 1

Taxing energy use: Introduction, scope and methodology

Effective tax rates on energy use translate statutory excise and carbon tax rates into rates per tonne of CO_2 and per GJ. For the Taxing Energy Use publications and database, effective tax rates on energy use are calculated for 42 OECD and G20 economies, distinguishing the main economic sectors and fuels used. This chapter describes the motivation and scope for the measurement and analysis of effective tax rates on energy use and carbon emissions from energy use. It also provides an overview of the methodology used and the data feeding into the calculation of effective tax rates. Some methodological refinements introduced for the second vintage of the Taxing Energy Use database are outlined, too.

The OECD collects data on specific taxes on energy use in all OECD countries and selected partner economies, and processes them to allow for systematic comparison of patterns of the taxation of energy use across countries. This report extracts the main insights from the second vintage of the database, which presents effective tax rates on energy use for 2015. The first *Taxing Energy Use* (TEU) vintage, with tax data for 2012, was discussed in *Taxing Energy Use: A Graphical Analysis* (OECD, 2013) and *Taxing Energy Use 2015: OECD and Selected Partner Economies* (OECD, 2015a). The first vintage is also the source of raw tax data used to construct *Effective Carbon Rates* (ECR, OECD, 2016), which discusses the state of carbon pricing, including specific taxes on energy use and emissions trading systems.

This report, which accompanies country notes that are published online, discusses the main insights from the TEU update. After discussing methodological refinements to the database in this chapter, Chapter 2 considers the landscape of taxes on energy use in 2015 and the main changes between 2012 and 2015. More specifically, Chapter 2 discusses carbon and other taxes on energy use by fuel, in different sectors, and highlights some differences between country groups. The report focusses on messages relating to the update, repeating only briefly discussions of motivation, scope and limitations that are discussed at greater length in previous TEU reports (OECD, 2013; OECD, 2015a).

The database of taxes on energy use covers OECD countries (34 in the first vintage, 35 in the second with the accession of Latvia in 2016) and 7 partner economies, namely Argentina, Brazil, China, India, Indonesia, Russia, and South Africa. Data on tax rates are for 2015, and these are combined with the most recent available data on energy use by fuel and sector, which are data obtained from the *Extended World Energy Balances* from the International Energy Agency pertaining to 2014 (IEA, 2016a). With its disaggregation of tax rates to the level of sectors and fuels, the TEU database is the most detailed and up-to-date database on energy taxation available.

The approach taken in TEU is to collect statutory rates by fuel and by sector, and to translate these into rates per unit of energy (EUR/GJ) and per unit of CO_2 emissions from energy use (EUR/tCO_2). The resulting rates are called effective tax rates. Taxes included are *specific* taxes on energy use, which in practice means mainly excise taxes and carbon taxes. Broadly applicable taxes, e.g. VAT or sales taxes, are not included, as the objective is to chart taxes that change the price of each type of energy use relative to the price of other expenditure items.

Specific taxes on energy use are the relevant ones to consider from an environmental pricing point of view, since these are the taxes that alter the relative prices of energy use and that can in principle be used to reflect marginal environmental damages. Some countries have introduced specific taxes on carbon with the explicit objective of mitigating carbon emissions, and some refer to environmental objectives to motivate relatively high excise taxes on energy use. Existing excise taxes are not always, and not even usually, primarily introduced for environmental purposes. As will be seen, this often results in poor alignment of taxes with environmental costs. Nevertheless, these taxes are specific to energy use, a form of consumption with environmentally relevant outcomes, so that the taxes are environmentally-related even if the policy intention behind their introduction is not.

The TEU database expresses tax rates on energy use in EUR/GJ and EUR/tCO_2. Taxes included are specific taxes on energy use (excise and carbon taxes). For fuels, the statutory base usually is volumetric, and conversion to GJ and CO_2 is straightforward given knowledge of the fuel type. For electricity as an energy carrier, taxes are either levied on generation fuels (input fuels) or on electricity use (kWh).

The tax rates from the database are summarised in energy tax profiles. These are available per country and for selected country groupings, and show tax rates across all fuels in six economic sectors: road transport, domestic off-road transport, industry, agriculture and fishing, residential and commercial, and electricity. On a country level, these energy tax profiles are available online only (in country notes); this report restricts discussion to energy tax profiles for country groups (see Chapter 2).

The first section of this chapter is a brief overview of the methodology used and the data feeding into the calculation of effective tax rates, and of how to read the energy tax profiles. More in-depth discussions are available in *Taxing Energy Use: A Graphical Analysis* (OECD, 2013) and *Taxing Energy Use 2015: OECD and Selected Partner Economies* (OECD, 2015a). The second section of this chapter explains some methodological refinements introduced for the second TEU vintage.

Structure of the energy tax profiles, methodology and data sources

The taxes included in the database are specific taxes on energy use, whether rates are quoted per-unit or as a percentage of the sales price (*ad valorem* taxes). To calculate effective tax rates on energy use, statutory tax rates are linked to energy use of a country, sourced from the IEA *Extended World Energy Balances*. The current (second) vintage links tax rates for 2015 to energy use for 2014 (the most recent available for use in the database for this companion document, IEA, 2016a). The first vintage linked 2012 tax rates to 2009 energy use.[1] For each country in the TEU Database, the energy tax profiles show the effective tax rates on different fuels in six economic sectors: road, off-road transport, industry, agriculture and fishing, the residential and commercial sector, and electricity.

The horizontal axis of the energy tax profiles plots a country's final energy use, including the net energy used in energy transport and the transformation of energy from one form into another (e.g. by refineries, from crude oil to diesel). Within each of the six economic sectors, fuel use is disaggregated in a way that reflects fuel use in a particular country. For example, if a country predominantly uses coal to generate electricity, the category showing the effective tax rate on coal will dominate the electricity sector, while all oil products are grouped together into a single category. Conversely, if a country primarily uses different oil products, fuel oil, diesel and LPG are shown separately.

Electricity and heat are different from the other types of energy use shown in the energy profiles, in that they are secondary energy products, produced using primary fuels as inputs. The basis for the calculation of effective tax rates, and the energy use and carbon emissions shown in the energy tax profiles, are the fuels used to produce electricity and heat (as opposed to the electricity and heat output generated from these fuels).

All energy use in each country is converted into common units of energy (GJ) and carbon emissions (tonnes of CO_2) using the standard conversion factors of the IPCC. Groupings of fuel types (e.g. oil and oil products, coal and coal gases) keep with the definitions of the documentation of the *Extended World Energy Balances* (IEA, 2016a). Energy tax profiles excluding carbon emissions from biomass from the horizontal axis are available online but are not discussed in this report.

The vertical axis of the energy tax profiles measures effective tax rates on energy use applicable at 1 April 2015. Taxes included are those which alter the relative prices of energy use, based on the principle that specific taxes can alter relative prices to reflect marginal environmental damages from using energy.

Carbon taxes, which typically set a tax rate on energy based on its carbon content, but which are often expressed per physical unit of energy for practical purposes are included, but the database also includes other specific taxes on energy use (primarily excise taxes), the rates of which are typically quoted per physical unit of energy. The tax rates employed in the analysis are obtained from country-specific sources, as detailed in the country notes accompanying the energy tax profiles, available online.

In Argentina, Indonesia and India, excise taxes are quoted as a percentage of the sales price, and these are translated into per-unit taxes using price information to allow for their inclusion into the database. Country-specific sources are listed in the country notes accompanying the database.

The database includes reduced tax rates that apply to specific fuels or uses. For example, where a country refunds all or part of an energy tax to specific industrial or agricultural users, this reduced rate is taken into account in the calculation of effective tax rates. In some cases, governments report these reduced rates as a tax expenditure, i.e. as a deviation from the "standard" tax rate. Where governments report such tax expenditures, the reduced rate is shown (in a lighter colour) in relation to the "benchmark" level of tax from which the reduced rate is considered a departure by the government in question. A key source of data on tax expenditures is the OECD *Inventory of Fossil Fuel Subsidies* (OECD, 2018, forthcoming) and the database associated with it. The latest data on tax expenditures reported by government available at the time of writing has been included in this vintage of the database, namely for 2014 (OECD, 2015b).

Carbon taxes and other taxes on energy use levied at subnational level are not included in the calculation of effective tax rates. Where important, energy taxes levied at the subnational level are indicated in a country's energy tax profile, for an illustrative group of states or provinces.

As explained in the next section of this chapter, taxes on electricity output are not included when ETRs are expressed in currency per tCO_2. When taxes on electricity output are included, i.e. when ETRs are expressed in currency per GJ, the taxes on electricity output are shown as though they applied directly to the fuels used to generate electricity (see *Taxing Energy Use: A Graphical Analysis*, OECD, 2013, for more detail).

Taxes which apply to a very broad range of goods, such as value added and retail sales taxes, are not included in the database, given that they generally do not change the relative prices of energy use. However, concessionary VAT or sales tax rates change relative prices, so should be accounted for in principle. However, data limitations currently prevent their inclusion on a comparable basis across the 42 countries covered. OECD (2015a) gauges the extent to which VAT rate differentiation takes place across OECD and G20 countries, and the OECD *Inventory of Fossil Fuel Subsidies* (OECD 2018, forthcoming) provides an estimate of the extent of revenue foregone from reduced VAT rates on energy products.

Useful comparison of taxes on energy use across countries requires that these taxes are added to a producer price of energy which broadly aligns with production costs. While this is a reasonable approximation of the situation in most of the countries under study, some countries apply price support measures which keep producer prices below production cost. Support measures for fossil fuels are not accounted for here, but a comprehensive estimate of revenue foregone and an in-depth discussion of their impacts can be found in the OECD *Inventory of Fossil Fuel Subsidies* and its Companion (OECD, 2018 forthcoming).

Methodological refinements

The methodological approach taken and the data sources used remain consistent across the two vintages of the TEU database, but some adjustments have been made to how the data is aggregated and presented. These changes are introduced to refine the estimates of the effective tax rates calculated, in particular in the industry sector, and to increase the comparability of the TEU data with the *Effective Carbon Rates* (OECD, 2016).

The adjustments concern the treatment of taxes on electricity output for the calculation of effective tax rates per tonne of CO_2, the grouping of energy use into economic sectors, the treatment of energy use and carbon emissions from the auto-generation of electricity in the industry sector, the presentation of carbon emissions from the combustion of biomass, and the treatment of carbon taxes in countries which also participate in an emissions trading system.

Taxes on electricity use

Taxes on electricity consumption, usually quoted per kWh, are a specific tax on energy use that alters the relative price of consuming electricity. These taxes are included in the TEU database, and were included in the calculation of effective tax rates in previous TEU publications (OECD, 2013 and 2015a), also when these effective tax rates were expressed per tonne of CO_2. This is no longer the case.

The effective tax rates on energy use continue to include price signals from taxes on electricity output when they are expressed in terms of their energy content, e.g. in EUR per GJ. When expressed in terms of carbon content, taxes on electricity output are no longer included.

Taxes on electricity output are independent of the fuel mix used to generate electricity and of the efficiency of generation. Taxes on electricity do induce users to become more electricity-efficient, but they do not send a direct price signal to discourage carbon-intensive generation. However, since effective tax rates per tonne of CO_2 are mainly interpreted as carbon taxes, and these are dominantly interpreted in the context of climate change mitigation policy instrument (CO_2 is not a neutral *numéraire*) it is better to exclude electricity output taxes from them.

Including taxes on electricity output would be appropriate if the carbon intensity of the electricity generation mix was essentially fixed. However, in fact, the carbon intensity of power generation is generally quite sensitive to carbon price signals. In the short term, the existence and magnitude of carbon taxes may, for instance, determine whether coal or gas-fired units are dispatched to meet demand (IEA, 2016b).

The result of excluding taxes on electricity output from effective tax rates expressed in currency per tCO_2 is that these rates are significantly lower in the electricity sector than those shown in earlier TEU publications and in *Effective Carbon Rates*. For ease of reference, the energy tax profiles published online are presented both including and excluding taxes on electricity output.

With respect to the coverage of (specific) taxes on electricity use, the database includes "compulsory, unrequited payments", in line with the OECD definition of the term (OECD, 2001). For comparison, this is a considerably more narrow definition than the one introduced in Regulation (EU) 2016/1952 on "European statistics on natural gas and electricity prices and repealing Directive 2008/92/EC" (European Commission, 2016). The latter defines a category "taxes, fees, levies and charges" which includes value added tax;

taxes, fees, levies or charges relating to the promotion of renewable energy sources, energy efficiency and CHP generation; those relating to capacity payments, energy security and generation adequacy and other required services; air quality and emissions charges; those relating to the nuclear sector; and finally all other taxes, fees, levies and charges.

These taxes, fees, levies and charges are part of the price of electricity use, and this part has been growing strongly in the European Union in recent years. Evidence presented in European Commission (2016) shows that the share of the taxes and levies component in household retail prices increased from 28% in 2008 to 38% in 2015. This increase is the consequence mainly of rising levies for renewable energy and combined heat and power. This component does not fall under the OECD definition of taxes, and is not included in the TEU database. Irrespective of views of the merit of precise classifications of electricity price components, this example highlights that the *tax* information in the TEU database does not capture all *price* movements, *in casu* it does not include costs related to renewable investment, also if these are part of retail prices.

Sector classification

The energy tax profiles shown in the previous TEU publications showed energy use for three broad sectors: transport, heating and process use, and electricity. Starting with this vintage, energy use is shown for six sectors: road, off-road transport, industry, agriculture and fishing, residential and commercial and electricity. These six sectors map to the three sectors previously used as shown in Table 1.1.

Table 1.1. **Sector classification of energy use**

3-sector classification	6-sector classification	Energy use grouped in these sectors
Transport	Road	All energy used in road transport
	Off-road	All energy used in off-road transport (incl. pipeline transport, rail, domestic aviation and maritime transport)
Heating & process use	Industry	All energy used in industrial processes, in heating (incl. inside industrial installations) and in the transformation of energy from one form into another (e.g. in refineries).
		Starting with the second vintage of the TEU database, this sector also includes emissions from the autogeneration of electricity (section 22.3).
	Commercial & residential	All energy used for commercial and residential heating
	Agriculture & fisheries	Energy used in agriculture, fisheries and forestry. Energy used in on-road transport in this sector is included in the road transport sector.
Electricity	Electricity	All fuels used to generate electricity in main generation (rather than the amount of electricity generated from each fuel).
		Fuels from autogeneration of electricity in industry are included with the industry sector.

The more detailed classification allows for a more precise picture of the taxation, particularly in the industry, the commercial and residential sector, and agriculture and fisheries sectors. The separation of fuels used in the road and off-road sectors allows appreciation of the different tax rates applying across the different fuels and uses in the broader transport sector. In addition, the grouping into six economic sectors is consistent with that of the *Effective Carbon Rates* report (OECD, 2016).

Energy use and emissions from the auto-generation of electricity

Electricity and heat can be produced as a main activity (main generation), or by (mostly) industrial or energy transformation users that also produce electricity on-site (auto-generation). The first vintage of the TEU database included auto-generation of electricity along with main generation.

However, for the calculation of *Effective Carbon Rates*, it was recognised that the accounting of emissions under emissions trading systems takes place at the facility level, so that when an industrial installation auto-generates heat or electricity, the emissions from that activity will be included with the emissions of the industrial sector. Emissions from auto-generated electricity accordingly were classified in the industrial sector. The same approach is now taken for the TEU database. As before, the data assumes that auto-generated electricity is taxed at the same rates as the electricity from main generation, which affects industry average rates. However, given that the shares of energy use and emissions from auto-generated electricity are relatively small in most countries, the resulting change in effective tax rates is minor.

Energy use and carbon emissions from biomass

Previous TEU publications did not explicitly differentiate the emissions from the combustion of biomass from other emissions from fuel combustion. However, in countries with a substantial proportion of biomass use, the energy tax profiles displayed biomass separately. In addition, effective tax rates on biofuels and waste were compared separately across countries.

In order to accommodate different approaches to accounting for the CO_2 emissions from biomass combustion, specifically those that treat biomass as carbon neutral on a life cycle basis, an additional energy tax profile (on a CO_2-basis) is published that excludes carbon emissions from the combustion of biomass, for all 42 countries. For most countries, the profiles with biomass combustion emissions "in" and "out" are very similar, but the differences are larger for, e.g. Brazil, Sweden and Switzerland. To avoid confusion, this report does not include this new tax profile, but it is published in the country notes online. Consistent with earlier publications, the effective tax rates shown in this report are calculated including carbon emissions from biomass.

Interactions between carbon taxes and emissions trading systems

Some countries that participate in or operate an emissions trading system refund carbon tax payments to the firms that are subject to these systems. Such interactions were noted in previous TEU publications and were sometimes taken into account by calculating a reduced effective tax rate on emissions in some industrial sectors.

The assumptions taken around the interactions between carbon taxes and emissions trading systems have now been refined using detailed information collected for the estimation of *Effective Carbon Rates* (OECD, 2016). Carbon taxes were fully, partially or not removed for the shares of energy use or emissions that are estimated as covered by an emissions trading system, in line with country approaches. Table 1.2 provides an overview of the adjustments made to carbon taxes where there is an emissions trading system.

Table 1.2. **Adjustments to carbon taxes made in sectors and fuels covered by ETS**

Jurisdiction	Treatment of carbon tax when ETS applies
Denmark	Fully removed
Finland	Not removed
France	Not removed
Ireland	Fully removed
Iceland	Not removed
Japan	Not removed
Latvia	Fully removed
Norway	Partially removed
Portugal	Fully removed
Slovenia	Not removed
Sweden	Fully removed
Switzerland	Fully removed
United Kingdom	Not removed

References

European Commission (2016), "Regulation (EU) 2016/1952 of the European Parliament and of the Council of 26 October 2016 on European statistics on natural gas and electricity prices and repealing Directive 2008/92/EC", *Official Journal of the European Union*, http://eur-lex.europa.eu/eli/reg/2016/1952/oj.

IEA (2016a), *Extended World Energy Balances* (database), www.iea.org/statistics/topics/energybalances.

IEA (2016b), *Medium-Term Coal Market Report 2016*, IEA, Paris, http://dx.doi.org/10.1787/mtrcoal-2016-en.

OECD (2018), *OECD Companion to the Inventory of Support Measures for Fossil Fuels 2018*, OECD Publishing, Paris.

OECD (2016), *Effective Carbon Rates: Pricing CO_2 through Taxes and Emissions Trading Systems*, OECD Publishing, Paris, http://dx.doi.org/10.1787/9789264260115-en.

OECD (2015a), *Taxing Energy Use 2015: OECD and Selected Partner Economies*, OECD Publishing, Paris, http://dx.doi.org/10.1787/9789264232334-en.

OECD (2015b), *OECD Inventory of Support Measures for Fossil Fuels* (database), www.oecd.org/site/tadffss/.

OECD (2013), *Taxing Energy Use: A Graphical Analysis*, OECD Publishing, Paris, http://dx.doi.org/10.1787/9789264183933-en.

OECD (2001), *OECD Glossary of Statistical Terms: Taxes*, https://stats.oecd.org/glossary/detail.asp?ID=2657.

Notes

1. Linking rates to use in an earlier year is obviously not ideal, but delays in the availability of energy use data and avoiding excessive lags in reporting tax data impose this choice. Internal analysis on the first vintage has revealed that the error from combining different years is small enough for it not to influence the type of insights discussed in this report. Future versions of the database will also combine tax and base data for the same year.

Chapter 2

Patterns of taxes on energy use and changes from 2012 to 2015

This chapter describes similarities among and differences between countries' profiles of taxes on energy use (energy and carbon taxes), by the main economic sectors and fuels used, for selected country groupings and on a country-by-country basis. The discussion focusses on tax rates expressed per tonne of CO_2. A main finding is the continued very poor alignment of taxes with the environment and climate costs of energy use, across all countries and country groups, though at different levels. Progress towards better use of taxes to cut harmful emissions is slow and piecemeal at best, and largely limited to the road sector.

The statistical data for Israel are supplied by and under the responsibility of the relevant Israeli authorities. The use of such data by the OECD is without prejudice to the status of the Golan Heights, East Jerusalem and Israeli settlements in the West Bank under the terms of international law.

This chapter describes similarities among, and differences between, countries' profiles of taxes on energy use, by different fuels, sectors and different country groupings. In addition, comparing 2015 rates to those of 2012, it identifies changes in taxing practice.

A main finding is the continued very poor alignment of taxes with the environment and climate costs of energy use, across all countries and country groups, though at different levels. Most taxes are well below where they should be to reflect climate costs alone, even using a very conservative estimate of the climate damage of EUR 30/tCO_2. Changes between 2012 and 2015 across the 42 countries are limited, and they mainly show in the road sector.

A few countries implemented tax reforms which contribute to enhancing the alignment of tax rates with the external costs of energy use both in the road and in the non-road sectors. However, with some exceptions, due to the weight of individual countries in the total, these reforms do not significantly change the overall pace of change, and misalignments remain.

By way of background, the first section of this chapter is an overview of the level and composition of energy use and carbon emissions from energy use across countries and sectors. The next section discusses the key features of effective tax rates by sector and fuel, across all countries and country groups, also focussing on comparing taxation in industry, the residential and commercial sector, and electricity. Next, the level and composition of effective tax rates on energy use in the road and non-road sectors are discussed, and effective tax rates are related to countries' broader economic characteristics. More specifically, effective tax rates are correlated with carbon emissions per unit of GDP per capita, the energy intensity of GDP and carbon intensity. The last section zooms in on the rates and coverage of carbon taxes in the countries which have introduced a specific tax on carbon.

The discussion focusses on tax rates expressed per tonne of CO_2. This does not reflect a view that taxes on energy use are or should be used only to price carbon emissions – indeed they also can be used, to an extent, to reflect environmental costs related to other emissions resulting from the combustion of fuels, and they can and do also serve revenue-raising functions. However, taxes on fossil fuels (or prices in emissions trading systems) are the ideal instrument to internalise external costs of CO_2 emissions, and the view is widely held that they (in combination with prices of tradable CO_2 emission permits) should at a minimum equal these external costs. Expressing tax rates in currency per tonne of CO_2 allows quick evaluation of whether they attain that objective.

This chapter often compares tax rates against a benchmark level of EUR 30 per tCO_2. In line with OECD work on *Effective Carbon Rates* (OECD, 2016) and thorough review of recent estimates, this value is taken as a lower-end estimate of the climate cost of CO_2 emissions. A more detailed discussion of this benchmark estimate can be found in Box 2.1 of this document, and Chapter 2 in OECD (2016).

To recall, the 42 countries included in the TEU database are the 35 OECD member countries (Latvia being a new member country since July 2016, it was not included in the first vintage of the database) and seven partner economies: Argentina, Brazil, China, India, Indonesia, Russia and South Africa. Among these, this section distinguishes between different country groupings. These are the 22 OECD member countries which are also part of the European Union, the 12 non-EU OECD member countries, and the seven partner economies.

Composition of and changes in energy use and carbon emissions from energy use

This section compares energy use and CO_2 emissions from energy use in the 42 countries in 2009, 2012 and 2014, the years which have been used to calculate effective tax rates on energy use in the different TEU and ECR publications.

Figure 2.1 shows that the 42 countries included in the TEU database account for just under 80% of world energy use. The share of energy use that the 42 countries collectively account for in 2014 is roughly the same as in 2009, but the composition within the group of 42 countries evolves. In particular, the share of OECD countries decreases over time, and that of the seven partner economies grows. In 2014, the seven partner economies account for a larger share of global energy use (39% in 2014, up from 35.4% in 2009) than then 35 OECD countries (38.5%, down from 42.8% in 2009), for the first time.

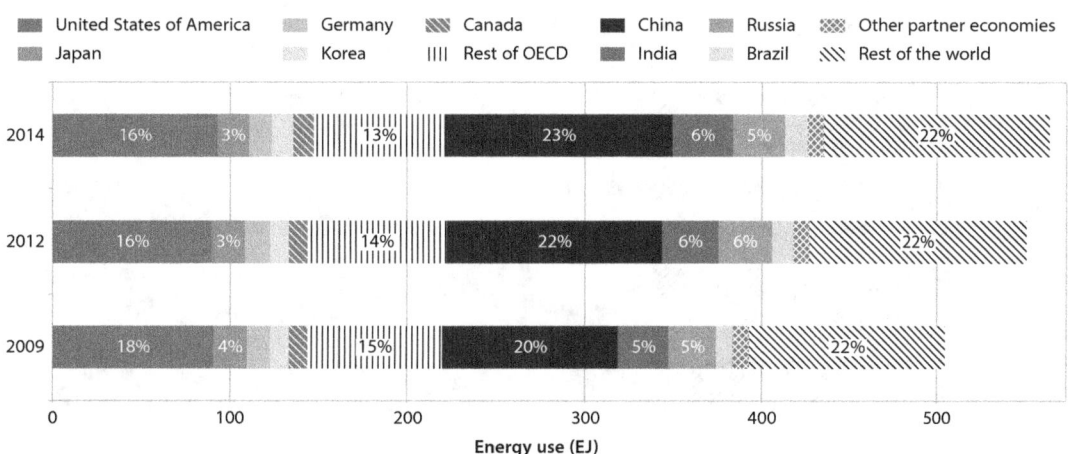

Figure 2.1. **Energy use by country or country groups in 2009, 2012 and 2014**

Notes: Individual countries are shown if their share in the total is at least 2%.

1 EJ = 1 000 000 TJ.

Source: Calculations based on *World Energy Balances* (IEA, 2016a).

Across the 42 countries, a few large countries account for the bulk of energy use, but here too relative weights are shifting. For example, in 2014, the United States accounted for 16.2% of energy use, down from 17.6% in 2009. China's share in world energy use amounts to 22.2% in 2014, up from 19.3% in 2009.

Overall, the growth in total energy use in 42 countries has been decelerating. Since 2010, energy use in the 42 countries has grown at 1.2% per year on average, down from an average yearly growth of 2.4% in the early 2000s. This deceleration is mainly caused by slower energy use growth in the seven partner economies, where energy use grew by 3.3% per year on average since 2010, down from 5.7% between 2000 and 2010.

At the sector level, across the 42 countries, carbon emissions from energy use are growing at the fastest pace in industry between 2009 and 2014. They rose by 15.3% between 2009 and 2012, and by 10.5% between 2012 and 2014. Carbon emissions from electricity generation grew by 18.6% between 2009 and 2012, but decreased by 2.2% between 2012 and 2014.

Emissions from outside of road transport tend to account for the bulk of emissions across all countries. Among these, the electricity, the industry and the residential and commercial sectors outweigh other non-road sectors in terms of their contribution to carbon emissions by far, in and across all countries. Road transport accounts for around 15% of carbon emissions from energy use across all countries.

Figure 2.2 shows that the distribution of carbon emissions from energy use differs between country groups. While the contribution of different sectors to total carbon emissions is roughly similar between the OECD-EU and non-EU OECD countries, the share of the industry sector in total carbon emissions is larger in the selected partner economies. Emissions from road transport are lower in the selected partner economies, but its share can be expected to grow quickly as per capita incomes rise further.

Figure 2.2. **Composition of CO_2 emissions from energy use by sector in different country groups, 2014, %**

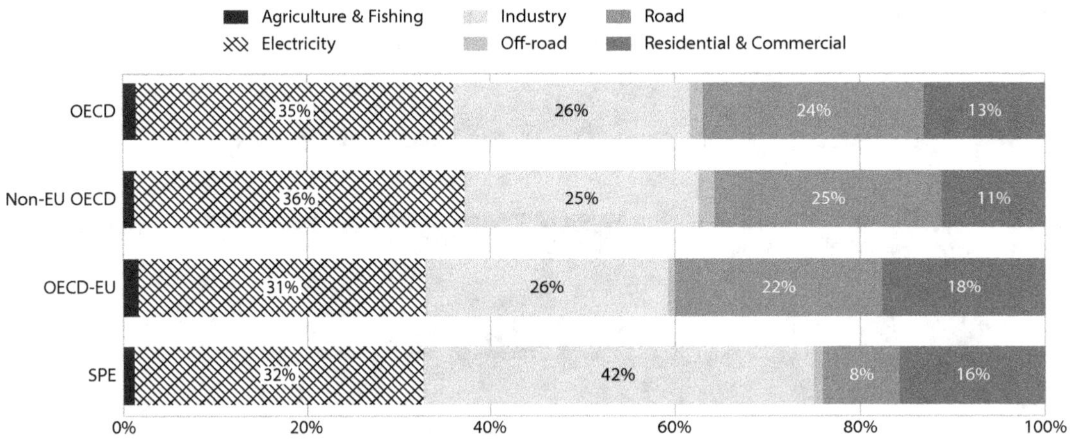

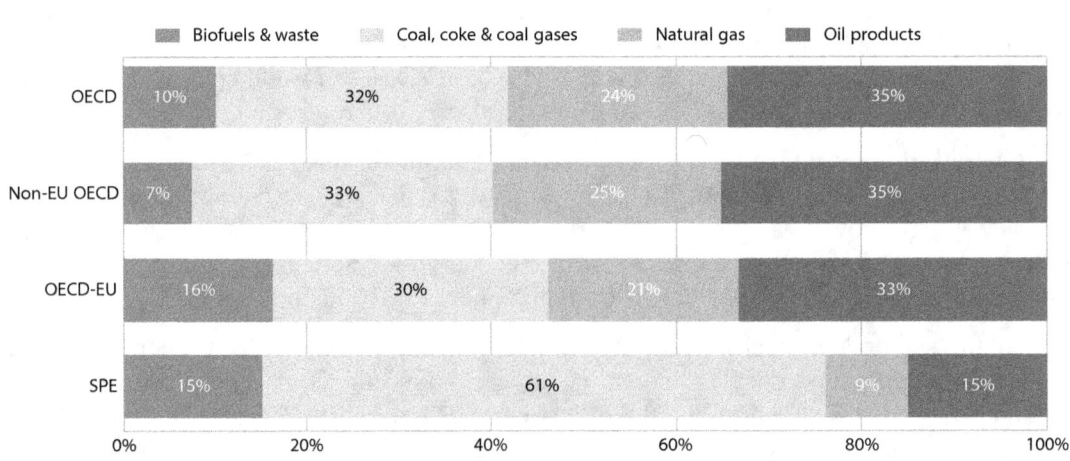

Source: Calculations based on *Extended World Energy Balances* (IEA, 2016b).

Figure 2.3. **Composition of CO_2 emissions from energy use by fuel for different country groups, 2014, %**

Source: Calculations based on *Extended World Energy Balances* (IEA, 2016b).

Figure 2.3 displays the shares of emissions from coal, oil products, biofuels and waste, and natural gas, again for the different country groups. As for sectors, shares are roughly similar across the OECD economies, but coal and coal products contribute a much larger share to emissions in the selected partner economies. Against this background, it is encouraging that global coal consumption in 2015 fell for the first time of the new millennium. Chinese coal consumption, which accounts for almost half of the global total, even fell for two years in a row but re-bounded recently (IEA, 2016c; Enerdata, 2018).

Effective tax rates – key features by fuel and by sector

This section provides an overview of the main patterns characterising the taxation of energy use in the 42 OECD and G20 economies across six economic sectors and different fuel types. It highlights the wide differences between tax rates on different fuel types and considers the large differences between tax rates on road and non-road sectors. The section also sheds light on the differences among effective tax rates in different country groupings.

The principal observations are that coal is taxed at the lowest rates per tonne of CO_2 by far, while oil products are taxed at the highest effective rates; taxes in the non-road sectors are below those in the road sector, by a factor of more than 20 across the 42 countries on average; taxes on energy use are higher in OECD EU countries than in other OECD countries and in OECD partner economies.

Taxes on energy use by fuel

Figure 2.4 breaks down the economy-wide effective tax rates in each country into effective tax rates on carbon emissions for each type of fossil fuel. The size of the circle for each fuel represents the share of that fuel in total carbon emissions of the country, and the economy-wide effective tax rate is also plotted.[1]

Immediately discernible from Figure 2.4 are the comparatively high rates applied to oil products compared to other fuels, in all countries included in the database. These high

Figure 2.4. **Effective tax rates on carbon emissions from energy use on each fuel in 2015 (biomass emissions included)**

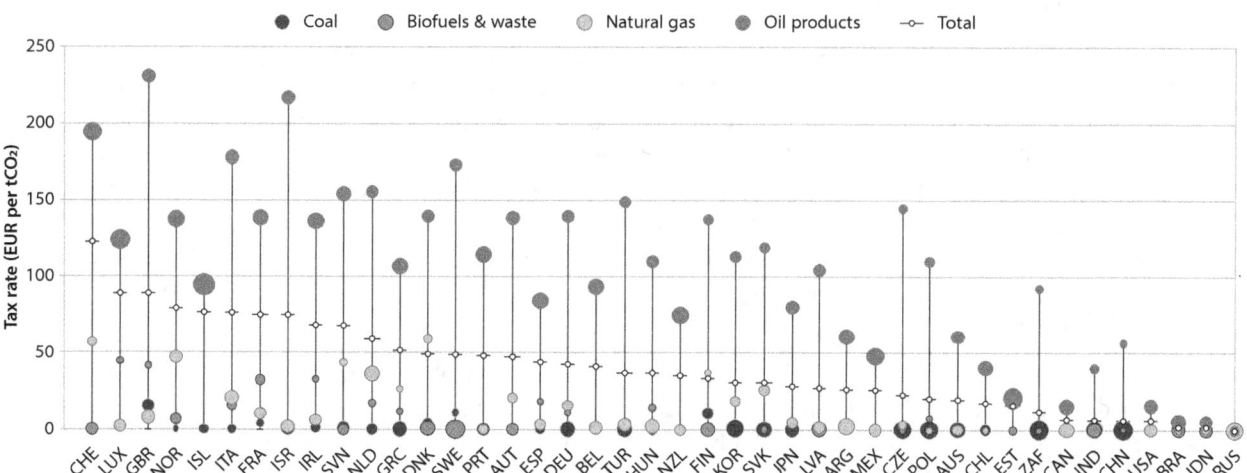

Note: Tax rates are shown as at 1 April 2015. Carbon emissions from energy use were calculated from data in the *Extended World Energy Balances* (IEA, 2016b).

rates are primarily, but not exclusively, the result of high taxes applied to fuels for road use. Coal, which contributes a significant share to carbon emissions in some countries, is taxed at much lower rates, and effective tax rates are zero or close to zero in the majority of countries.

The taxation patterns for each fuel have remained broadly stable between 2012 and 2015, but some changes in the tax rates by fuels can be highlighted at the country level. For example, in India, the Clean Energy Cess, which applies to all coal, lignite and peat use, was increased from INR 50 per tonne in 2012 to INR 200 per tonne in 2015,[2] and a new tax on bituminous coal was introduced in Korea. These changes are visible in the energy tax profiles of the two countries, but the rates at which these taxes applied in 2015 remain too low to make a large difference in Figure 2.4 or in the aggregate figures shown in forthcoming sections.

Comparing by fuel group, the change in the taxation of oil products is largest, and its effects are concentrated in the road sector. Compared to 2012, large increases in the tax rates on oil products were implemented in China, Mexico and India. This will be discussed below.

Taxes on energy use in road transport compared to other sectors

Overall, taxes on energy use are relatively high in road transport, whereas rates exceed EUR 30 per tCO_2 for a very small share of non-transport emissions only. This picture is fairly stable across both years, except for substantial increases in tax rates on road fuels rates in the middle of the distribution.

Figure 2.5 plots the proportion of carbon emissions subject to different levels of effective tax rates, in EUR per tCO_2 in the road sector (in panel A) and the non-road sectors (in panel B), with tax rates for 2012 and 2015. The horizontal axes of each figure sorts emissions from the lowest to the highest taxed, with the range normalised to 100% to allow comparison of the distributions over time and between sectors. The vertical axis shows the tax rates.

A first observation is that effective tax rates are strongly heterogeneous in both years and for both sector classifications shown. This implies that it is not very helpful to think in terms of average rates across all sectors, as this average hides large differences in actually applicable rates.

Nearly all carbon emissions from road transport are taxed, and they are taxed at relatively high rates. In 2015, 97% of emissions from road transport are taxed, and 91% are taxed above EUR 5 per tCO_2. Rates exceed EUR 30 per tCO_2 for 50% of emissions, and EUR 50 per tCO_2 for 47%. Comparing across years, the most discernible change in the effective tax rates in road transport is an increase in rates in the middle of the distribution. In particular, the share of emissions taxed above EUR 30 per tCO_2 increased from 46% in 2012 to 50% in 2015, and rates exceed EUR 50 per tCO_2 for 47% of emissions in 2015, compared to 37% in 2012. However, other, smaller changes are observed, too, and go in both directions.

However, as discussed in Box 2.1, due to the range of other external costs from road transport, "higher" rates in this sector does not necessarily imply that the rates are "high enough", even if rates are considerably higher than EUR 30per tCO_2. EUR 30 per tCO_2 is a conservative estimate of the climate cost of a tonne of CO_2 emissions, and is in that sense a minimum rate that should be reached if taxes on energy use were used for climate policy purposes only. The partial evidence discussed in Box 2.1 suggests that excise on road fuels is near the low end of estimates of external costs related to fuel use, in two countries featuring among the highest effective tax rates across the 42 countries covered. In essence, this suggests that in most cases the relatively high transport fuel taxes are still too low from an environmental point of view.

The distribution of tax rates in non-road sectors features a long tail with rates equal to or close to zero, and a very small share of emissions subject to higher rates, across both years. In 2015, excluding taxes on electricity output, 81% of emissions are not taxed, 92% are taxed at below EUR 5 per tCO_2 and just 3% are taxed above EUR 30 per tCO_2. The next section outlines taxation patterns across country groups, followed by two subsections which disaggregate the changes in rates in the road and non-road sectors on a country level.

Figure 2.5. **Proportion of carbon emissions from energy use subject to different levels of effective tax rates in the road and non-road sectors, in 2012 and 2015 (excluding taxes on electricity output, including carbon emissions from biomass)**

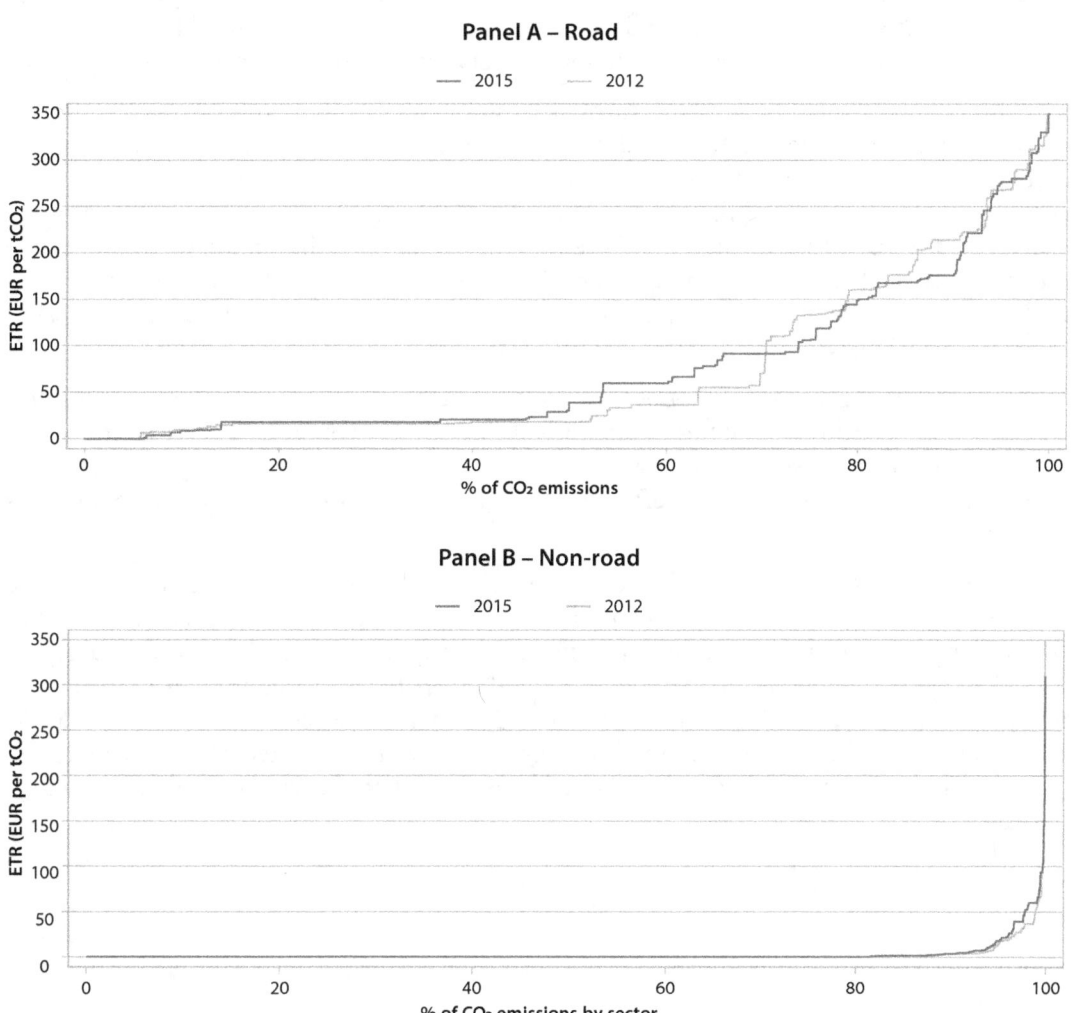

Note: All tax rates are expressed in 2012 prices. Carbon emissions from energy use were calculated from data in the *Extended World Energy Balances* (IEA, 2016b).

Taxes on energy use by fuel and sector in different country groups

The energy tax profiles discussed here summarise the taxation of energy use for different groups of countries. The groups are the 42 countries (Figure 2.6), all OECD countries (Figure 2.7), all OECD countries which are also EU members (Figure 2.8), all non-EU OECD countries (Figure 2.9) and the seven selected partner economies (Figure 2.10).

In each of the energy tax profiles, effective tax rates from energy taxes are plotted in EUR per tCO_2 along the vertical axis, and emissions from energy use in 1000 tCO_2 are shown along the horizontal axis. Carbon emissions are grouped into six economic sectors and by the main fuels. Scales are adapted to improve legibility of the profiles, so they differ between the figures.

The profiles include carbon emissions from biomass, they are either separately identified or grouped with carbon emissions from waste. Figures 2.6 through 2.10 exclude taxes on electricity output from the calculation of effective tax rates. The energy tax profiles distinguish between carbon taxes and other taxes on energy use, via the black horizontal lines across the blue bars. More methodological detail is included in Chapter 1.

The energy tax profiles differ substantially among country groups, both in terms of effective tax rates across fuels and sectors, as well as in terms of the composition of carbon emissions from energy use. The highest overall tax rates are observed in the OECD countries which are also EU members (Figure 2.8). In this group, energy taxes are strongly shaped by the 2003 Energy Taxation Directive, which sets minimum tax rates for a wide range of fuels in different economic sectors. Tax rates are significantly lower in the non-EU OECD countries (Figure 2.9), both in the road and non-road sectors, and rates are lowest in the seven OECD key partners group (Figure 2.10).

In all country groups, oil product use in the road sector is taxed at the highest rates. Biofuels also tend to be taxed at comparatively high rates when used in road transport. However, this is because many countries tax their use at the same statutory rates as fossil fuels, which translates into high effective tax rates due to the lower carbon content of biofuels.

Within the road sector, the differential taxation of gasoline and diesel is identifiable in all energy tax profiles, but the magnitude and direction varies between country groups. In the non-EU OECD countries, on a weighted average basis, diesel is taxed at a higher effective rate per tonne of CO_2 than gasoline, and this pattern also dominates in the Figure for the group of the OECD countries (Figure 2.7) and for all countries (Figure 2.6). In the group of the EU-OECD countries (Figure 2.8) and the selected partner economies (Figure 2.10), gasoline is taxed at a higher effective rate than diesel, on a weighted average basis.

2. PATTERNS OF TAXES ON ENERGY USE AND CHANGES FROM 2012 TO 2015 – 31

Figure 2.6. **Effective tax rates on energy use in the 42 OECD and G20 economies in EUR/tCO$_2$, 2015** (excluding taxes on electricity output, including carbon emissions from biomass)

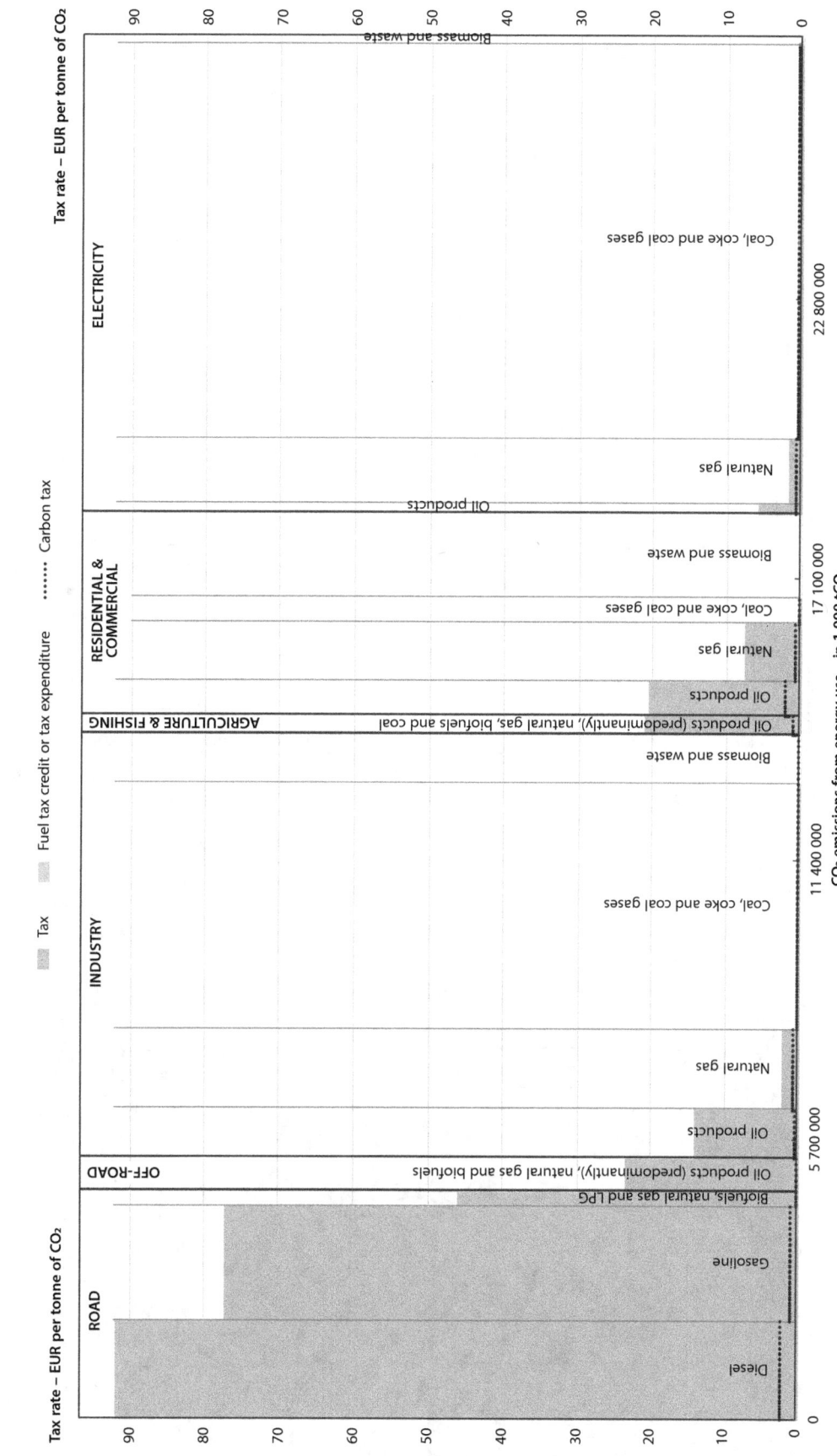

Note: Tax rates are shown as at 1 April 2015. Carbon emissions from energy use were calculated from data in the *Extended World Energy Balances* (IEA, 2016b).

32 – 2. PATTERNS OF TAXES ON ENERGY USE AND CHANGES FROM 2012 TO 2015

Figure 2.7. **Effective tax rates on energy use in OECD countries in EUR/tCO$_2$, 2015 (excluding taxes on electricity output, including carbon emissions from biomass)**

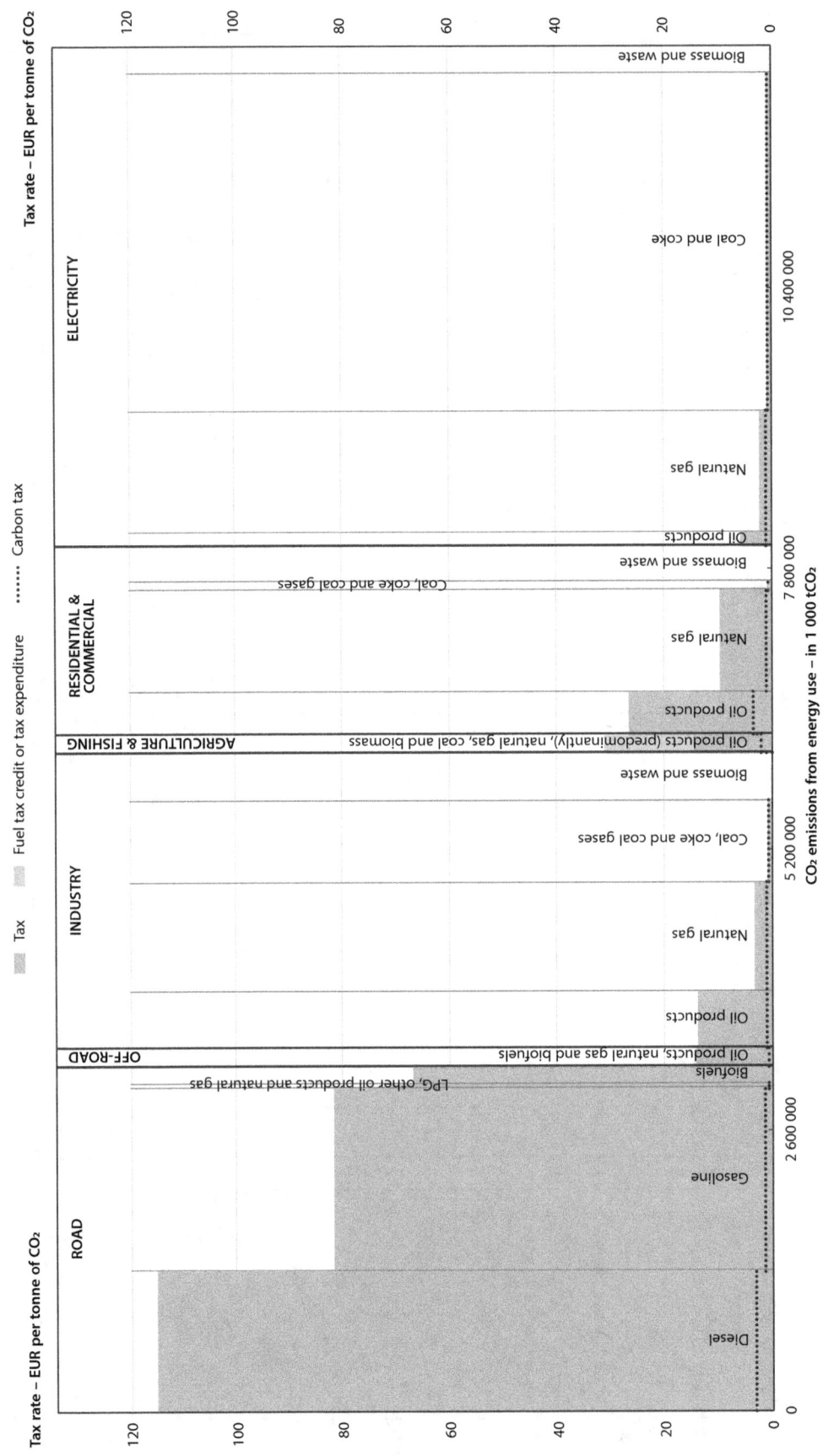

Note: Tax rates are shown as at 1 April 2015. Carbon emissions from energy use were calculated from data in the *Extended World Energy Balances* (IEA, 2016b).

2. PATTERNS OF TAXES ON ENERGY USE AND CHANGES FROM 2012 TO 2015 – 33

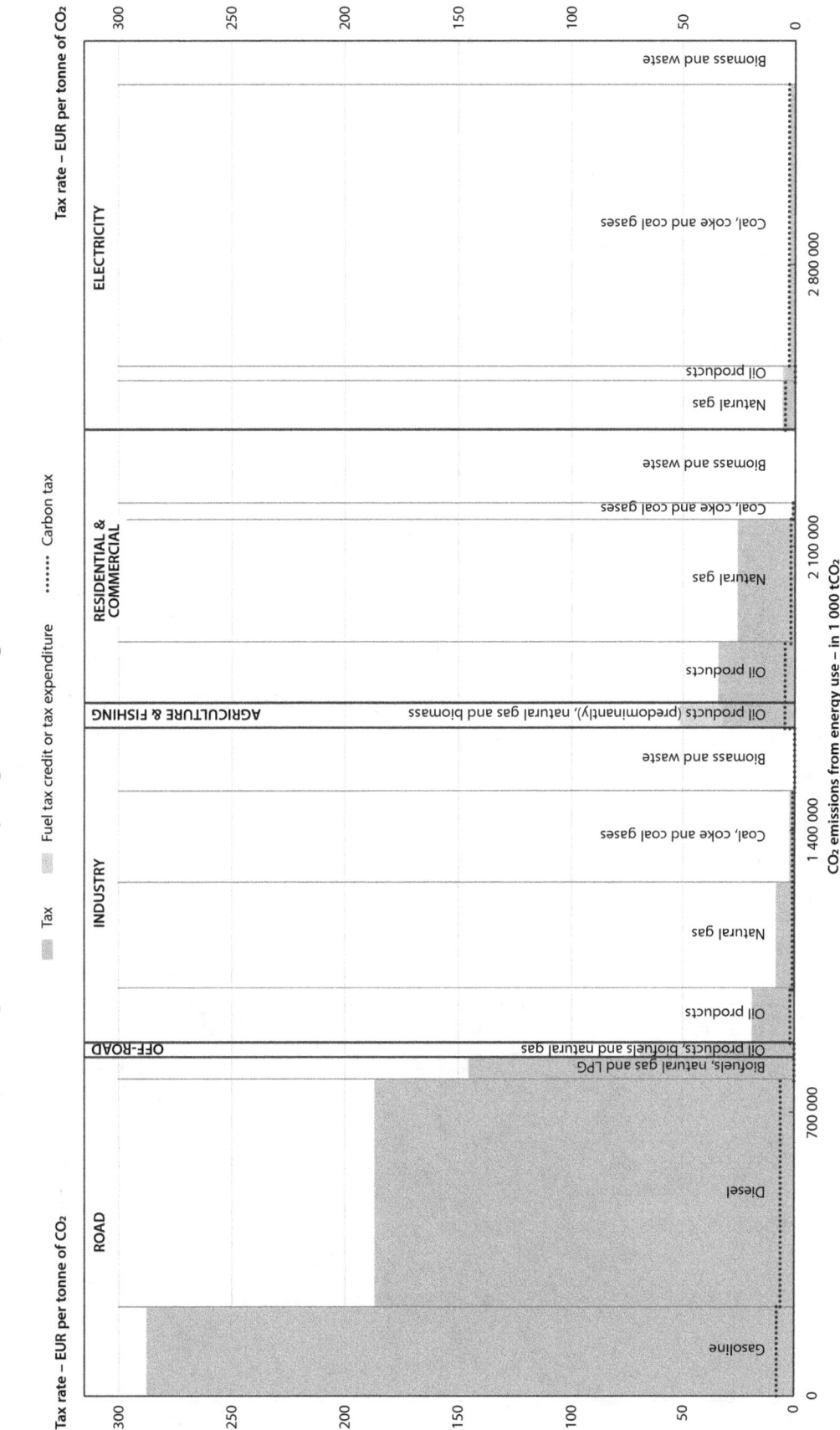

Figure 2.8. **Effective tax rates on energy use in the 22 OECD economies that are also members of the European Union in EUR/tCO$_2$, 2015 (excluding taxes on electricity output, including carbon emissions from biomass)**

Note: Tax rates are shown as at 1 April 2015. Carbon emissions from energy use were calculated from data in the *Extended World Energy Balances* (IEA, 2016b).

34 – 2. PATTERNS OF TAXES ON ENERGY USE AND CHANGES FROM 2012 TO 2015

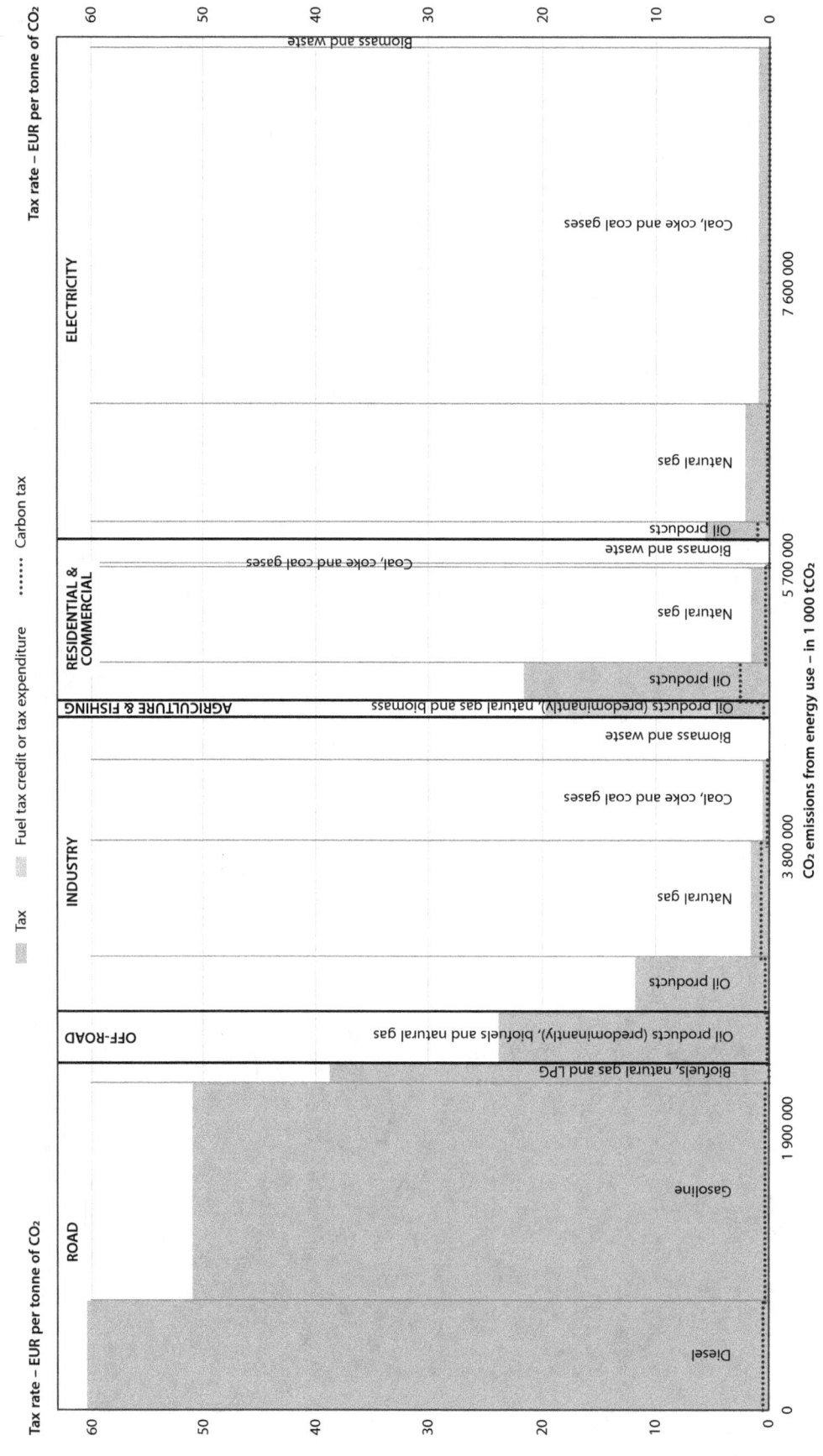

Figure 2.9. **Effective tax rates on energy use in non-EU OECD economies in EUR/tCO$_2$, 2015 (excluding taxes on electricity output, including carbon emissions from biomass)**

Note: Tax rates are shown as at 1 April 2015. Carbon emissions from energy use were calculated from data in the *Extended World Energy Balances* (IEA, 2016b).

2. PATTERNS OF TAXES ON ENERGY USE AND CHANGES FROM 2012 TO 2015 – 35

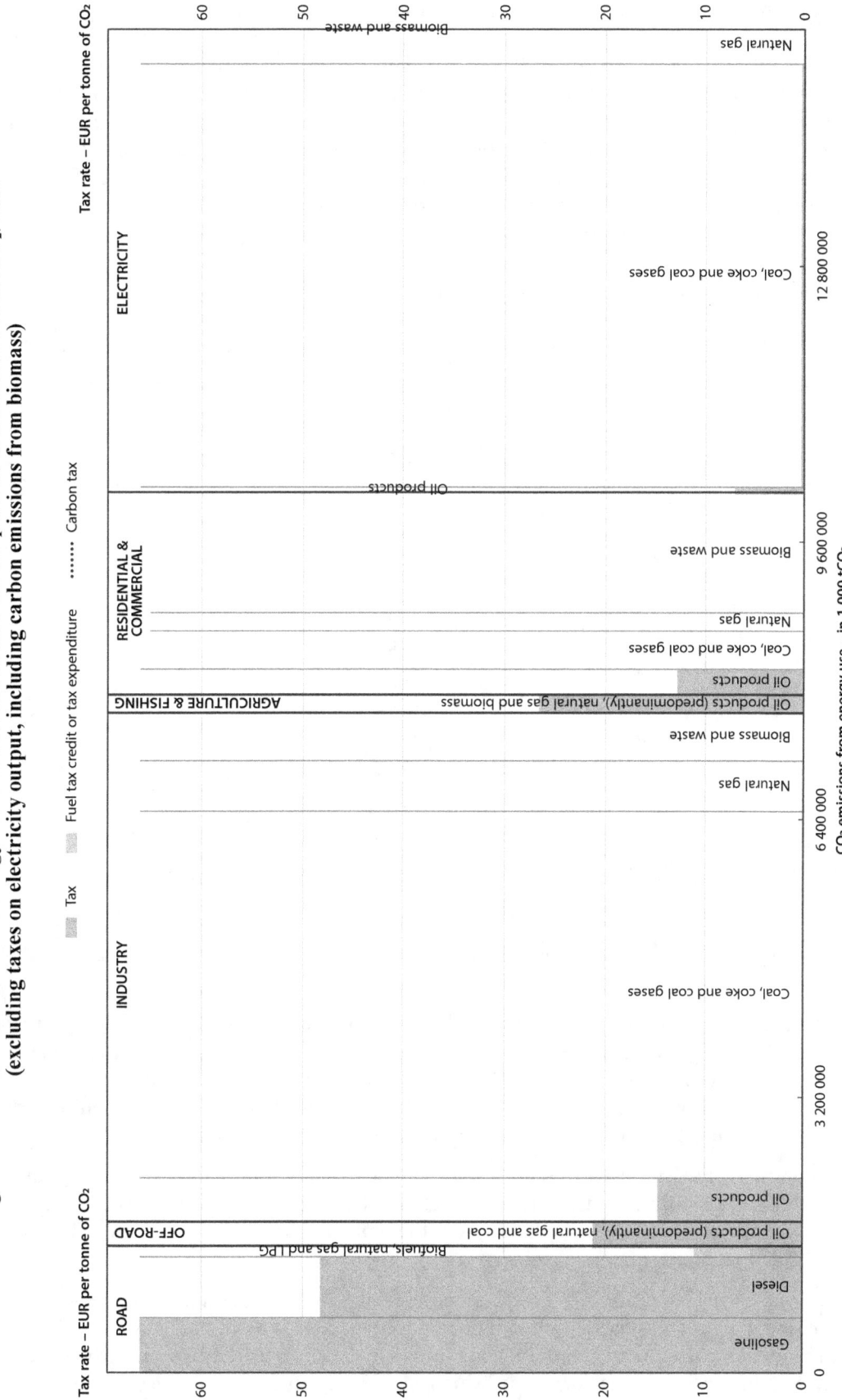

Figure 2.10. **Effective tax rates on energy use in the seven selected OECD partner economies in EUR/tCO$_2$, 2015**
(excluding taxes on electricity output, including carbon emissions from biomass)

Note: Tax rates are shown as at 1 April 2015. Carbon emissions from energy use were calculated from data in the *Extended World Energy Balances* (IEA, 2016b).

Given that 40 out of the 42 countries tax diesel at a lower effective rate than gasoline, it may be surprising that, on a weighted average basis, the effective tax rate on diesel is higher than that on gasoline across all countries and for some country groups (OECD and non-EU OECD). This result is due to the weight of some large non-EU OECD countries in the total weighted average tax rates. Table 2.1 illustrates the shares of carbon emissions from gasoline and diesel in individual countries in the total, thus indicating the weight of their respective tax rates on gasoline and diesel in determining the total average effective tax rate on gasoline and diesel for road use across all countries. The next section of this chapter discusses the differential taxation of gasoline and diesel by country.

Table 2.1. **Share of a countries gasoline, diesel and road sector emissions in total, %, 2014**

Country	Gasoline share in total gasoline emissions, road	Diesel share in total diesel emissions, road	Road sector emissions in total emissions from road
USA	45.1%	20.7%	33.8%
CHN	12.2%	15.5%	13.7%
JPN	5.2%	3.2%	4.0%
RUS	4.72%	2.0%	3.2%
MEX	4.32%	2.1%	3.1%
CAN	3.96%	2.4%	3.1%
BRA	3.2%	5.7%	5.1%
IDN	3.04%	2.6%	2.6%
IND	2.5%	7.6%	4.6%
DEU	2.2%	4.8%	3.4%
FRA	0.8%	4.9%	2.7%
GBR	1.6%	3.6%	2.4%
ITA	1.1%	3.4%	2.2%
ESP	0.56%	3.1%	1.6%
KOR	1.14%	2.4%	1.9%
TUR	0.24%	2.1%	1.1%

Note: Countries are shown if their share of diesel or gasoline emissions in total diesel or gasoline emissions from the road sector exceeds 2%, the table is ordered by countries' share of gasoline emissions. Carbon emissions from energy use were calculated from data in the *Extended World Energy Balances* (IEA, 2016b).

Tax rates are much lower in the non-road sectors than in the road sector, in all country groupings, and the gaps between effective tax rates on different fuels per tonne of carbon are wide. Oil products are always taxed at the highest rates, natural gas is taxed at lower rates and coal, which accounts for major shares of carbon emissions in the main non-road sectors (though to different extents between the country groups), is taxed at very low or zero rates.

Among the three main non-road sectors (residential and commercial, industry, and electricity), fuels are taxed at the highest effective rates in the residential and commercial sector. On average across all fuels, tax rates in the industry sector are about half as high as in the residential and commercial sector.

Both in the EU and non-EU OECD countries, the higher taxation of the residential and commercial sector is partly due to higher statutory rates than in industry. In addition, countries which participate in an ETS and which also levy specific taxes on carbon often cancel carbon tax payments for firms which participate in a trading system, lowering effective tax rates in industry. Conversely, carbon taxes apply more strongly to fuels used in the residential and commercial sector. However, permit prices in emissions trading systems have been relatively low, such that they do not make up for the difference in taxation between the industry and the residential and commercial sector.

Input fuels for electricity generation are almost never taxed, leading to an effective tax rate of close to zero in all country groupings. On environmental grounds, the absence of taxes on fuels used to generate electricity inputs is particularly counterproductive, since electricity still depends very strongly on carbon-intensive fuels. The rates are low across all country groupings, but the disparity between the taxation of the electricity and other sectors is larger in EU countries.

In the European Union, according to the Energy Tax Directive, Member States shall exempt from taxation energy products and electricity when used to produce electricity. The Directive allows Member States to apply a tax to the fuels used to generate electricity, for environmental reasons, and without having to respect the minimum levels of taxation laid down in the Directive. However, not many countries make use of that provision. One of the exceptions is Italy, where the fuels used to generate electricity are taxed, at relatively low rates when compared to the rates which are applied to fuel use in other sectors. The Energy Tax Directive regulates the taxation of electricity output instead. However, taxes on electricity output do not send a direct price signal to discourage carbon-intensive or inefficient generation, which is why they are excluded when effective tax rates are expressed in currency per tCO_2, as in Figures 2.6-2.10.

To improve readability, Figures 2.6-2.10 show off-road transport as a single fuel use category. In all of the country groups, off-road transport is mainly composed of oil products used for domestic rail, aviation and marine transport. While many countries tax fuel use in off-road transport at the same rates as road transport fuels in principle, almost all countries grant reduced tax rates or exemptions to domestic off-road transport fuels. These tend to be reported as tax expenditures. International transport fuel consumption, which is tax-exempt by international conventions, is not included in the profiles.

Fuel use in agriculture and fishing is dominated by oil products, which are typically subject to high rates, but derogations from the full tax rates are often provided when fuels are used in this sector.

Effective tax rates in the road sector by country

The first subsection of this chapter pointed to relatively high tax rates in road transport. This section breaks these rates down by tax instrument, and discusses changes in rates by country.

Figure 2.11 shows average effective tax rates on carbon emissions from energy use in the road sector, distinguishing price signals from carbon taxes and from excise taxes and notes changes in average rates between 2012 and 2015. Carbon taxes on road transport fuels are used in a few countries only, and usually form a small share of the full effective tax rate. Effective tax rates in the road sector are predominantly from excise taxes on road fuels.

Figure 2.11 also reveals which countries drive the change in effective tax rates shown in Figure 2.5, which shows the proportion of carbon emissions from energy use subject to different levels of effective tax rates in the road and non-road sectors, in 2012 and 2015. At lower tax rates, changes are driven by changes in Canada, Indonesia, Russia and the United States. The larger changes in the middle range are the result of fuel pricing reforms in China, India and Mexico. At higher tax rates, the changes stem mainly from tax rate movements in European countries.

Figure 2.11. **Average effective tax rates from excise taxes and specific taxes on carbon by country in the road sector, in EUR/tCO$_2$, 2015 and 2012**

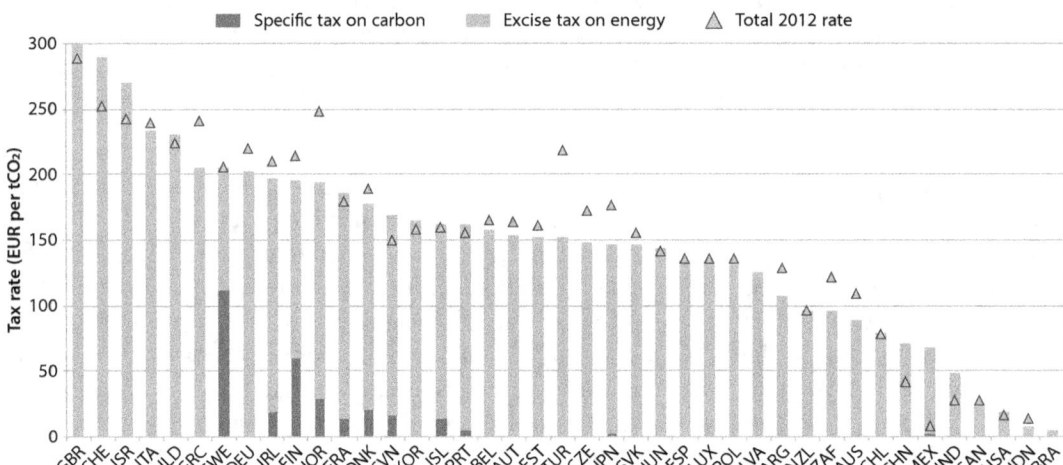

Note: All tax rates are expressed in 2012 prices. Due a lack of price data, Argentina was excluded from comparisons of tax rates across years. Since Latvia was not included in previous vintages of the database, data are available only for 2015. Effective tax rates are calculated including the carbon emissions from biomass. For countries with a currency other than the Euro, changes in effective tax rates can differ when expressed in local currency (see Figure 12.2 for changes in local currency units).

While average effective tax rates increased or remained stable in some countries over time, they decreased in others. Changes in effective tax rates (in EUR per tCO$_2$) can be the result of changes in the statutory tax rate, or changes in the carbon intensity of the tax base. In addition, for countries with a different currency than the Euro, changes in rates between two years can also be the result of exchange rate fluctuations. In most countries, inflation contributes to changes in effective rates, too, though some countries (e.g. Australia, Chile, Denmark, the Netherlands, Norway and Sweden, and the United Kingdom until 2013) compensate the real decrease in nominal rates by automatically indexing statutory tax rates for inflation (Mahler et al. 2017).[3] The following paragraphs briefly highlight where either of the components played a particularly strong role in driving the change in effective tax rates in road transport in individual countries.

Although increases in the statutory rate play a role, the increase in effective rates in the middle of the distribution shown in Figure 2.5 is also a consequence of China's increasing share of total emissions across all countries (as its emissions are taxed at middle range rates). The same is true for India, where increases in carbon emissions amplify rate increases, though the pace of emissions increase has not been as strong (6.4% between 2012 and 2014 in the road sector). While changes in the country shares of the carbon emissions base affect the distribution of effective tax rates, this base effect is dominated by rate changes and changes in the composition of the fuel mix within the sector.

For tax rates expressed in Euros, exchange rate fluctuations over time also affect tax rates for countries not part of the Euro area. For example, real effective tax rates can increase in local currency but may remain unchanged or decline when quoted in Euros. It is therefore useful to consider change over time in national currency. To account for these differences, Figure 2.12 plots the changes in effective tax rates in local currency units. In addition, the online country notes show effective tax rates in local currency units.

Figure 2.12. **Percentage change in average effective tax rates in the road sector by country in local currency units, 2012-15**

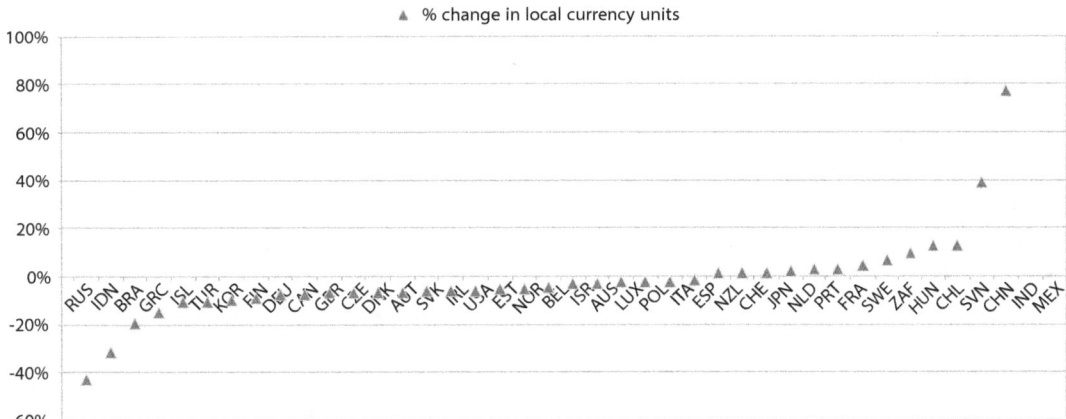

Notes: Percentage change is indicated in 2012 prices per local currency units. The change in Mexico's average effective tax rates between 2012 and 2015 is 724%. To improve legibility, Mexico is not shown. Due a lack of price data, Argentina was excluded from comparisons of tax rates across years. Since Latvia was not included in previous vintages of the database, data are shown only for 2015. Effective tax rates are calculated including the carbon emissions from biomass.

In the case of Switzerland, for example, the appreciation of the local currency against the Euro between 2012 and 2015 makes the change in the effective tax rate larger in Euros than in national currency. On the contrary, in Chile real domestic rates have increased more strongly in national currency than in Euros. Exchange rate fluctuations reverse the direction of effective tax rate changes in the case of the United Kingdom, Israel, Korea, Sweden and South Africa. Specifically, rates increase in national currency but decrease when quoted in Euros in the cases of Sweden, and South Africa; and rates decrease in national currency compared to an increase in Euros, and from a domestic decrease to an increase in the United Kingdom, Israel and Korea.

Within the road sector, there are large differences in effective tax rates between gasoline and diesel, the two main fuels used in road transport. At the current state of equipment and technology, diesel usually emits higher levels of harmful air pollutants per litre than gasoline, and also the carbon content of diesel per litre is higher. This suggests that on environmental grounds diesel should be taxed at rates which are at least as high as those of gasoline (see e.g. Harding, 2014 for more detail).

Figure 2.13 shows the effective tax rates on gasoline and diesel for road use in 2015, ordered by countries' effective tax rates on gasoline. Contrary to what environmental policy considerations would suggest, diesel is taxed at lower effective rates than gasoline in all of the countries studied, except in the United States and Mexico. Note that in both latter countries, the tax rates on both gasoline and diesel are at the lower end of the distribution across all countries. In both Mexico and the United States, reliance on gasoline for fuel use in the road sector is relatively strong (68.5% and 66.9%, respectively). In the United States, almost all of the (lower-taxed) gasoline is used by passenger cars and light trucks, while heavy goods vehicles tend to run on (higher-taxed) diesel (United States Department of Transportation, 2015). This is in contrast to the situation on many European countries, where heavy transport is often taxed at lower rates.

Figure 2.13. **Effective tax rates on gasoline and diesel for road use in EUR/tCO$_2$ in 2015**

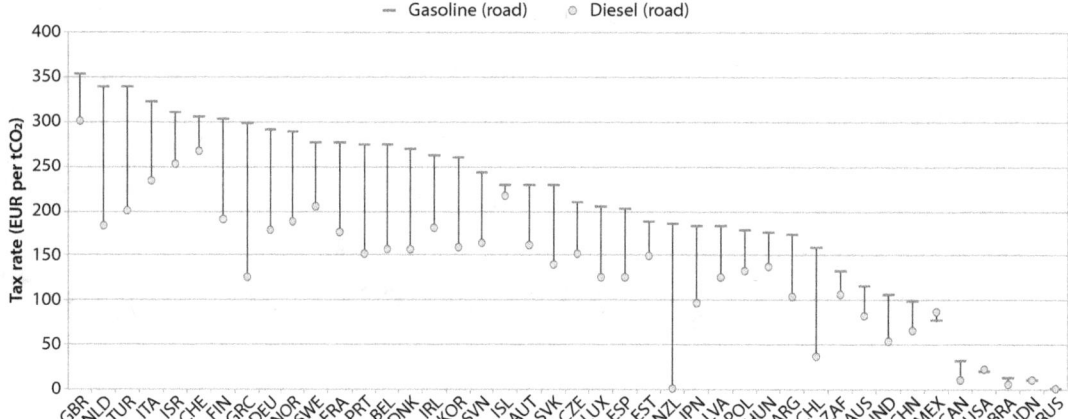

Notes: Tax rates are shown as at 1 April 2015. Carbon emissions from energy use were calculated from data in the *Extended World Energy Balances* (2016b). For countries with a currency other than the Euro, changes in effective tax rates can differ when expressed in local currency (see Figure 2.14 for changes in local currency units).

The gap between the effective tax rates on gasoline and diesel is particularly large in the case of New Zealand, but this is an artefact reflecting New Zealand's particular tax structure. New Zealand taxes gasoline for road use through an excise tax, but not diesel. Instead, diesel cars pay distance-based charges ("Road User Charges", RUC). Since road user charges affect different behavioural margins than a tax on fuel use (e.g. distance-based charges do not create a direct incentive to economise on fuel use), they are not included in the TEU database and do not appear in Figure 2.13.[4]

As in relation to Figure 2.11, for countries with a currency other than the Euro, exchange rate fluctuations play a role for determining effective tax rates on gasoline and diesel when quoted in EUR per tCO$_2$. To account for these, Figure 2.14 plots the percentage change in the gap between effective tax rates on gasoline and diesel in local currency units, between 2012 and 2015. Though the gap between effective tax rates remains wide in the majority of countries, it has been narrowing in most across the time period analysed.

Mexico has made the narrowing of the differential taxation of gasoline and diesel an explicit objective of its energy tax reform, which has been rolled out gradually over the past years (Arlinghaus and Van Dender, 2016). A few other countries are implementing policies to narrow the "diesel differential", but not all of the effects of the reforms show in the data included in this report yet, due a lag in data availability (see Chapter 1 for methodological details).

Figure 2.14. **Percentage change in the gap between the effective tax rate on gasoline and diesel between 2012 and 2015**

Notes: Percentage change is indicated in 2012 prices per local currency units. Effective tax rates are calculated including the carbon emissions from biomass. Mexico has narrowed the gap between its effective tax rate on gasoline and diesel by 464% between 2012 and 2015. To improve legibility, Mexico is not shown. Due a lack of price data, Argentina was excluded from comparisons of tax rates across years. Since Latvia was not included in previous vintages of the database, data are shown only for 2015.

Box 2.1. **What is an appropriate benchmark for taxes on energy use?**

The economically optimal level of taxes on energy use is difficult to establish, like for any other tax or policy variable. The view taken in OECD work on environmental taxation (e.g. OECD, 2017) is that taxes and other market-based instruments (e.g. emissions trading systems) should reflect the environmental costs and any other damage associated with energy use, i.e. they should reflect marginal external costs.

Optimal tax levels are also influenced by other considerations, e.g. related to revenue-raising, to equity and to competitiveness. Adapting taxes for equity and competitiveness reasons is often done in practice, but is not ideal as other more suitable instruments are available for providing compensation without compromising effectiveness.

The impact of revenue-raising objectives on optimal tax levels is empirically difficult to establish, but different models indicate that the marginal economic cost of tax distortions is lower for environmentally related taxes than for labour taxes (e.g. Groothuis, 2016). This would imply that an equal revenue tax shift from labour taxes to taxes on energy use, e.g. by aligning taxes on energy use with the external costs of energy use, reduces the overall economic cost of raising the given amount of revenue. Note that considerations related to revenue-raising are unrelated to the funding needs in a particular sector. Imposing sector-specific budget constraints can potentially be useful for regulatory or political economy reasons (not considered in this report) but are not productive from a public finance point of view.

As a rule of thumb, therefore, tax reform should aim for closer alignment of taxes and prices of tradable permits with the costs of negative impacts of energy use. Practical implementation of this rule of thumb is difficult, however, as it requires evidence on the relevant external costs, which – with some exceptions – is not readily available. The alternative approach, adopted in this report, is to establish a minimum requirement: if price signals from

> **Box 2.1. What is an appropriate benchmark for taxes on energy use?** *(continued)*
>
> market-based instruments were used to reflect external costs from CO_2 emissions only, then they should not be lower than a low-end estimate of these external costs, namely EUR 30/tCO_2. This is a relevant criterion given the large gaps that currently exist between price signals and the EUR 30/tCO_2 minimum, in all sectors studied, except road transport.
>
> Effective tax rates are well above EUR 30/tCO_2 in road transport in many countries. Does this mean that they are high enough? Not necessarily. First, EUR 30/tCO_2 is a conservative estimate of climate damages from CO_2 emissions, so higher rates are likely justified for climate reasons alone: EUR 30/tCO_2 is truly a minimum. Second, taxes can play a broader role than reflecting climate costs alone. This is true for taxes in all sectors, and very much so in transport because of the high external costs of mainly air pollution, accidents and congestion. While detailed information on the level of these costs is not at hand for all countries, some rough indications can be extracted from Van Dender (2018, forthcoming), which itself builds on sources from the European Union, France and the United Kingdom, by way of example.
>
> On the basis of these back-of-the-envelope calculations, Figure 2.15 shows the sum of marginal external costs associated with a litre of fuel use, for France and the United Kingdom, averaged across gasoline and diesel and distinguishing between urban and rural driving. As can be seen, in the two leftmost columns, the external costs are much larger for urban driving. This is mainly because of higher congestion costs, and to a lesser extent because of greater exposure to air pollution.
>
> In order to compare excise taxes with external costs, to know if they are approximately aligned, the external costs of congestion need to be adjusted downwards to account for the fact that car users respond to higher fuel taxes partly by driving less (which reduces congestion) but also by investing more in fuel economy (which does not reduce congestion). Since evidence indicates that both responses are about equally large in the long run, the adjustment factor for congestion costs is 50%, as an order of magnitude. The scaled down external costs estimates are shown in the third and fourth column of the figure, labelled "mec-ft" (for marginal external costs relevant to fuel tax comparison).
>
> The adjusted marginal external costs can be compared to the prevailing excise taxes. Keeping in mind that both sets of numbers (taxes and marginal external costs) are estimates, the insight is that excise taxes appear to be fairly well aligned with the marginal external costs of rural driving, and well below those of urban driving.
>
> Are fuel excise taxes then on average too low? Since the main difference between urban and rural driving pertains to congestion costs, and since congestion costs in rural driving are very low, the answer to this question depends on one's view on how congestion costs are best dealt with. As explained in more detail in Van Dender (2018, forthcoming), fuel taxes are not very well suited for curbing congestion, and electronic charging mechanisms that at least allow for better internalisation of external costs of congestion are increasingly being deployed. If, however, the view is that more sophisticated congestion pricing or other congestion management policies remain elusive, then higher fuel taxes appear to be justified on the basis of the estimates presented in the figure.
>
> However, to allow for better congestion management and also anticipating on eventual decarbonisation of road transport, it may be better to argue for more sophisticated congestion pricing than for increasing fuel taxes to reflect average congestion. Fuel taxes then would be "about right" on the basis of Figure 2.15. At this point, however, it is worth noting that the marginal external cost estimates used for Figure 2.15 should be considered as low end estimates, particularly for air pollution where they are based on assumed compliance with emission standards.

Box 2.1. **What is an appropriate benchmark for taxes on energy use?** *(continued)*

In sum, since excise taxes appear to align with low end estimates of marginal external costs, and since they are in the vicinity of marginal external costs only where congestion costs are very low, current fuel taxes in France and the United Kingdom are at the low end of appropriate levels, suggesting that moderate increases are likely to engender further social benefits. If fuel taxes are thought to have a role in curbing congestion, then they at present appear to be too low. These results are similar to those of a more comprehensive exercise for EU countries (Santos, 2017).

Figure 2.15. **Estimates of marginal external costs and of fuel excise tax, France and United Kingdom, EUR/litre of gasoline and diesel**

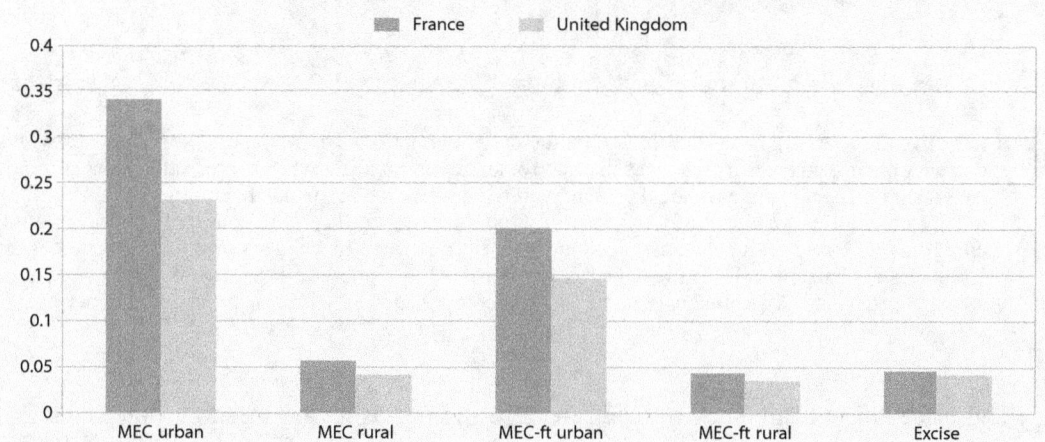

Legend: **MEC** = marginal external cost; **urban** = driving in urban environments; **MEC-ft** = MEC as relevant to the fuel tax, i.e. after correction for indirect impact of fuel costs on driving-related eternal costs; **rural** = driving in rural environments (to be understood as non-urban).

Source: Based on Van Dender (2018, forthcoming).

Effective tax rates in non-road sectors by country

This section takes a closer look at the level and composition of effective tax rates outside of road transport, as well as their change between 2012 and 2015 in the 42 countries.

The tax rates shown for the non-road sector include the industry, residential and commercial and the electricity sectors, as well as off-road transport and agriculture and fishing. As pointed out earlier in this chapter, the contribution of off-road transport and agriculture and fishing to total carbon emissions on energy use is very small, making their contribution to the effective tax rates averaged across the different non-road sectors negligible.

Compared to previous vintages of the TEU data, the data shown in this section exclude taxes on electricity output when quoting tax rates per tonne of carbon. Since most taxes on electricity are in fact output taxes, this leads to lower average effective tax rates across the non-road sectors. Figure 2.16 shows the average effective tax rates per tonne of CO_2 across non-road sectors in the 42 countries. The rates are below EUR 30 per tCO_2 in all but two of the countries studied, and below EUR 5 per tCO_2 in most.

Figure 2.16. **Average effective tax rates from excise taxes and specific taxes on carbon by country across the non-road sectors, in EUR/tCO$_2$, 2015 and 2012 (including carbon emissions from biomass)**

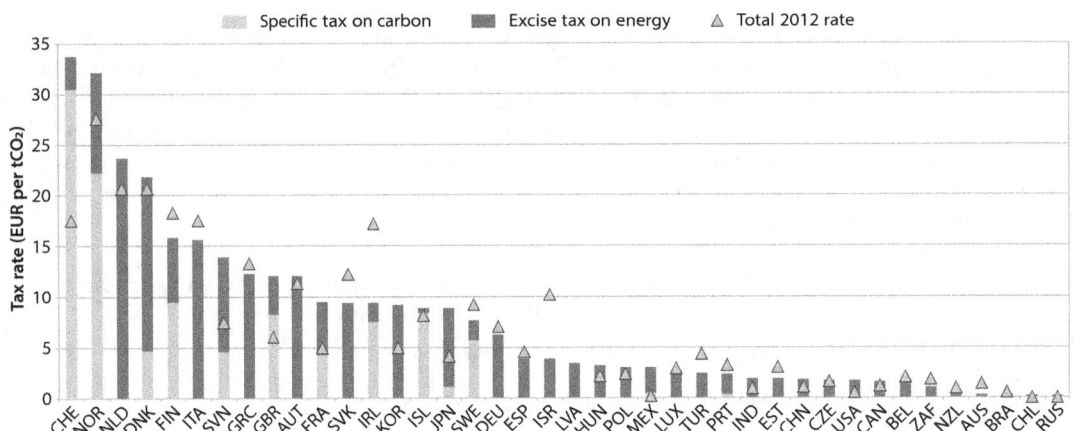

Notes: Effective tax rates are calculated including the carbon emissions from biomass. For countries with a currency other than the Euro, changes in effective tax rates can differ when expressed in local currency (see Figure 2.17 for changes in local currency units). As detailed in the documentation of IEA (2016b), energy use figures for Israel rely on a set of assumptions specific to the country. Starting in 2013, energy use is based on a new classification system. Consequently, changes in effective tax rates for Israel reflect changes in the estimated emissions base. All tax rates are expressed in 2012 prices. Due a lack of price data, Argentina was excluded from comparisons of tax rates across years. Since Latvia was not included in previous vintages of the database, data are shown only for 2015.

The effective tax rate shown in Figure 2.16 distinguishes between carbon taxes and other specific taxes on energy use. Excise taxes are by far the largest component of the effective tax rates across non-road sectors, but carbon taxes are a much more significant component in non-road sectors than in road transport. In 2015, thirteen of the 42 countries in the TEU database tax energy via a specific tax on carbon, most of these countries also tax carbon emissions in non-road sectors at relatively high rates. The design and coverage of national carbon taxes which apply in the countries included in the TEU database is discussed further in the last section of this chapter.

Figure 2.16 also reveals that, though there have been significant changes in effective tax rates in the non-road sectors in a few countries between 2012 and 2015, trends in the sense of systematically increasing or decreasing rates are not clearly identifiable. In many EU countries, statutory rates remained unchanged between the two years, which translates in to real rate decreases over time. In proportion to their initial rates, tax rate increases are highest in China, India, Japan, Korea and Mexico, many of which countries with initially low rates.

As also discussed in relation to Figure 2.11, changes in effective rates are shaped by changes in statutory rates, in carbon emissions, and exchange rate fluctuations. Since statutory tax rates have changed less strongly in the non-road sectors than in the road sector and rates are lower, changes in the emissions base influence the swings in effective tax rates more strongly across countries. However, in particular in China, France, India, Japan, Korea, Mexico and the United Kingdom, the tax rate increases outweigh movements in the emissions base.

Again, to account for changes in exchange rates influencing ETRs per tCO$_2$, Figure 2.17 shows real changes in effective rates in the non-road sectors in countries' local currency units, in percent. While the magnitude of change differs across the different countries, exchange rate movements do not reverse the direction of the change in any country.

Eroded rates by inflation also play a role outside of the road sector, but due to low rates, the extent of change is smaller than in the road sector.

Figure 2.17. **Percentage change in average effective tax rates in the non-road sector by country in local currency units, 2012-15**

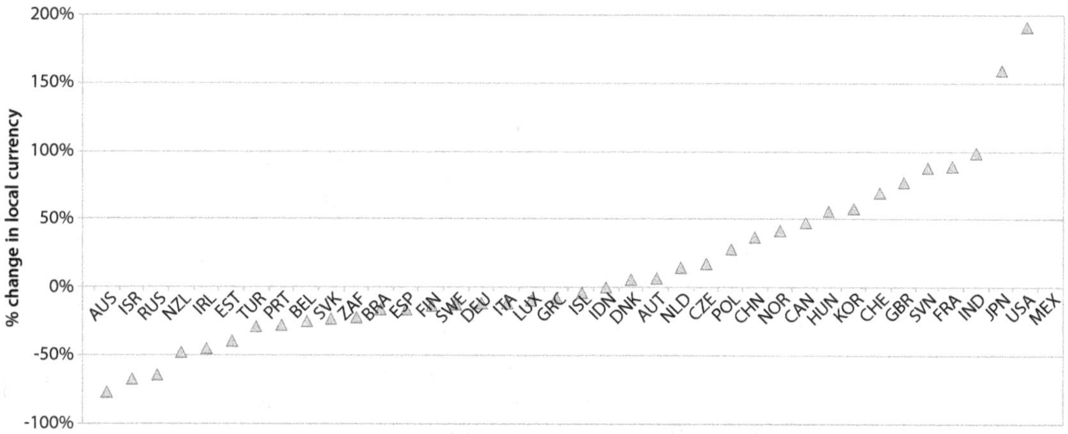

Notes: Percentage change is indicated in 2012 prices per local currency units. Effective tax rates are calculated including the carbon emissions from biomass. The change in Mexico's average effective tax rates between 2012 and 2015 is 1271.5%. To improve legibility, Mexico is not shown. As detailed in the documentation of IEA (2016b), energy use figures for Israel rely on a set of assumptions specific to the country. Starting in 2013, energy use is based on a new classification system. Consequently, changes in effective tax rates for Israel reflect changes in the estimated emissions base. Due a lack of price data, Argentina was excluded from comparisons of tax rates across years. Since Latvia was not included in previous vintages of the database, data exist only for 2015.

ETRs and countries' broader economic characteristics

Relating average effective tax rates to broader economic characteristics can help make sense of the large differences in rates across countries. Figures 2.18 to 2.20 plot country-level average effective tax rates per tonne of CO_2 against carbon emissions per unit of GDP per capita, carbon intensity of energy use and the energy intensity of GDP, respectively.[5] It is important, however, to keep in mind that such correlations do not imply a causal relationship between variables.

Figure 2.18 shows that the correlation between the country-level average effective tax rates on CO_2 emissions from energy use and GDP per capita is positive. Countries with higher per capita income tend to be characterised by higher average rates. The dispersion is generally quite large, especially among countries with relatively low average effective tax rates.

Several high-income European countries are shown to have very high average effective rates, also since the EU Energy Taxation Directive shapes how EU member states tax energy. However, Luxembourg has a very high effective tax rate compared to the relatively low statutory tax rate it levies levied compared to other EU countries. The explanation is that due to Luxembourg's central geographic location, the low statutory rates compared to neighbouring countries attract fuel tourism and boost sales to transit traffic. The dataset accounts for these emissions as domestic energy use, given lack of data on where the energy is actually consumed. As a result, the road sector, with high effective tax rates compared to other sectors, represents a disproportionate share in the countries' CO_2 emissions, inflating the country's average effective tax rate.

Figure 2.18. **Average effective tax rates on CO_2 emissions from energy use and GDP per capita**

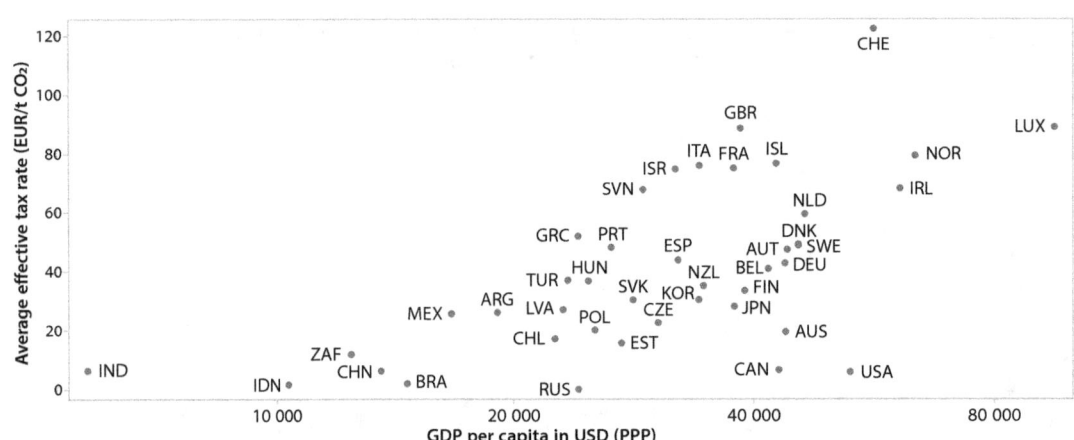

Notes: Tax rates are shown as at 1 April 2015. Carbon emissions from energy use were calculated from data in the *Extended World Energy Balances* (IEA, 2016b). Data on GDP per capita is from the *World Development Indicators* (World Bank, 2017). Effective tax rates are calculated including the carbon emissions from biomass.

Another noteworthy cluster comprises the Eastern European countries, whose average effective rates tend to be lower than the rates of other EU member states. While also statutory rates tend to be somewhat lower on average in Eastern European countries than in the rest of the EU, these differences are also the result of different energy profiles – economies at lower levels of GDP tend to use relatively more energy in industry as opposed to transport. Given that statutory and effective tax rates are higher in road transport, this lowers a country's average effective rates, everything else being equal.

Similarly, while sector-level effective tax rates are generally higher in OECD countries than in OECD partner economies (e.g. Figures 2.6-2.10), differences in country-level effective tax rates are somewhat overstated, considering that energy profiles are closely related to a country's level of economic development.

Figure 2.19 relates average effective tax rates on CO_2 emissions from energy use to the carbon intensity of energy use, showing a negative relationship between the two variables. However, effective tax rates vary widely between countries with a very similar carbon intensity of the energy mix, suggesting that other energy policies and energy supply conditions play a strong role in shaping a countries' carbon intensity of energy use.

While causality could go in either direction, it remains worth noting that countries which use primarily carbon-free fuels (e.g. renewables or nuclear) also tend to apply relatively high effective tax rates on carbon, and the carbon intensity of the energy mix tends to be higher in countries with lower effective tax rates on carbon.

Higher taxes on energy use provide energy users with a signal to use energy more efficiently. To the extent that energy taxes are higher for more carbon-intensive fuels, they also provide an incentive to reduce the carbon intensity of production. Figure 2.20 plots effective tax rates on carbon emissions from energy use against the energy intensity of GDP. The figure shows that more energy-intensive economies tend to feature lower average effective tax rates on energy use.

Figure 2.19. **Average effective tax rates on CO_2 from energy and carbon intensity of energy use**

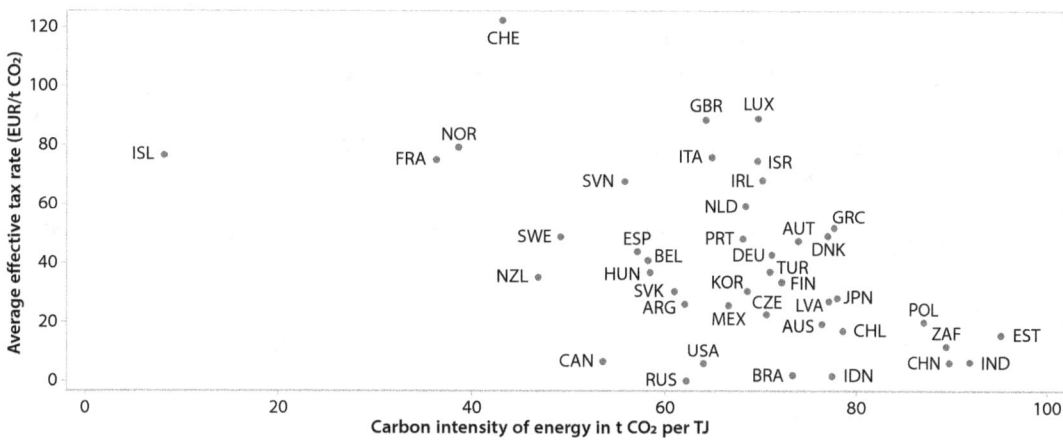

Notes: Tax rates are shown as at 1 April 2015. Carbon emissions from energy use were calculated from data in the *Extended World Energy Balances* (IEA, 2016b). GDP data is from the *World Development Indicators* (World Bank, 2017). Effective tax rates are calculated including the carbon emissions from biomass.

Figure 2.20. **Average effective tax rates on CO_2 from energy and energy intensity of GDP**

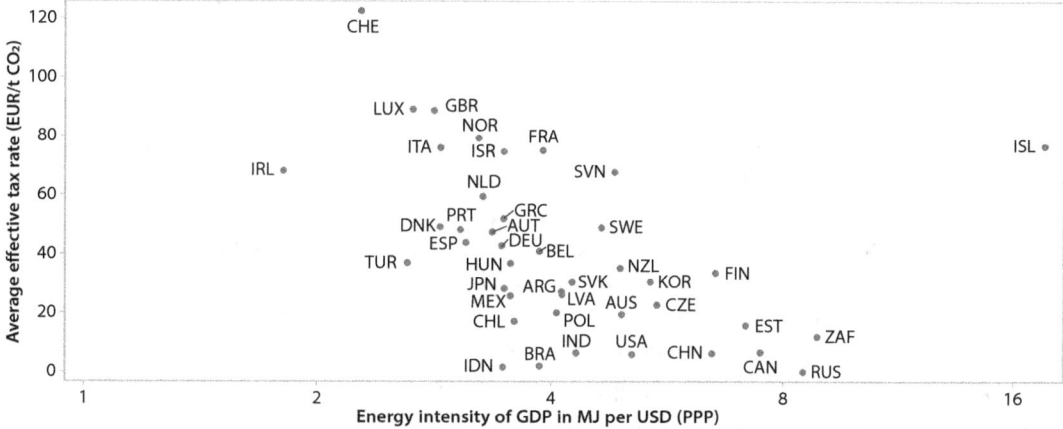

Notes: Tax rates are shown as at 1 April 2015. Carbon emissions from energy use were calculated from data in the *Extended World Energy Balances* (IEA, 2016b). GDP data is from the *World Development Indicators* (World Bank, 2017). Effective tax rates are calculated including the carbon emissions from biomass.

Carbon taxes by sector and fuel

An increasing number of countries are introducing specific taxes on carbon. In contrast to other excise taxes on energy use, the rates of which are quoted in currency per unit of energy (e.g. per litre or tonne), the rates of specific taxes on carbon are usually quoted in per tonne of carbon. While these taxes have existed in many Northern European countries since the 1990s, France, Ireland, Japan, Mexico and Portugal have newly introduced specific taxes on carbon in recent years. Where they exist at national level, these taxes are included in the *Taxing Energy Use* database.[6]

Some countries explicitly mention these taxes as a means to reach the pledges made in their nationally determined contributions to reaching the target they collectively agreed upon in the Paris Agreement on climate change, namely that of limiting the increase in worldwide temperatures to well below 2° C above pre-industrial times.

Figure 2.21 plots the share of carbon emissions from energy use in the 42 countries against the amount of emissions taxed under a carbon tax at different rates, in 2012 and 2015. The share of emissions that is subject to a carbon tax has increased, but remains low at just 5%. Across all countries only 0.3% of emissions at an effective carbon tax rate exceeding EUR 30 per tCO_2, indicating that where they apply, the rates of carbon taxes are low. Due to their limited reach and modest rates, the impact of carbon taxes on abatement seems to remain limited to date.

Figure 2.21. **Proportion of CO_2 emissions from energy use subject to different levels of effective tax rates from carbon taxes (biomass emissions included)**

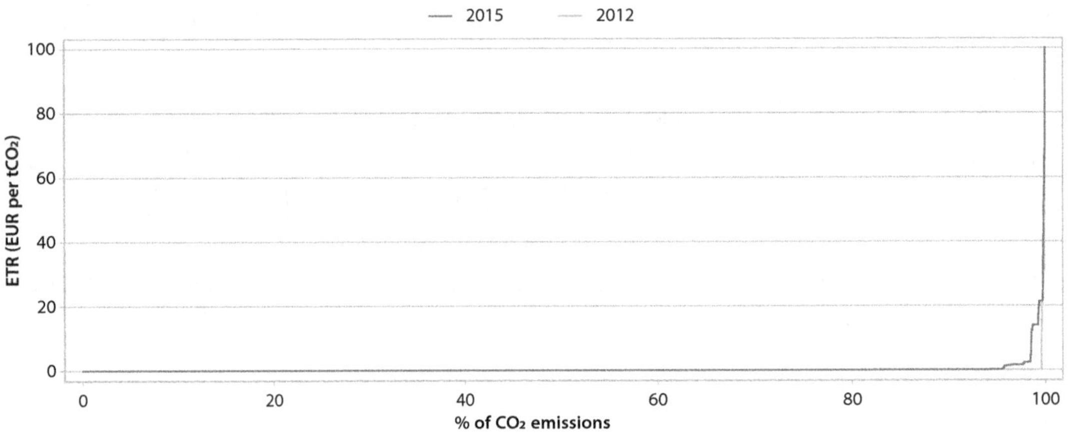

Notes: Tax rates are shown as at 1 April 2015. Carbon emissions from energy use were calculated from data in the *Extended World Energy Balances* (IEA, 2016b).

In many of the countries which have introduced a carbon tax, these taxes apply to less than 50% of carbon emissions from energy use, and rates vary widely. This is shown in Figure 2.22, which plots carbon tax rates in percent of the total amount of carbon emissions in each country that has introduced a carbon tax in the different panels.

While carbon taxes ideally are uniform per unit of CO_2 emissions, irrespective of fuel or sector, practical tax design often deviates from this intention. Carbon taxes are often set per unit of fuel instead of per unit of CO_2 emissions, so rates can and do vary across sectors and fuels.

Efforts to harmonise carbon prices across energy users have led many countries to restrict carbon taxes to non-ETS sectors, e.g. firms which are too small for inclusion in an ETS, or energy users in the residential and commercial sectors. In practice, however, the low permit prices prevalent in trading systems have meant that carbon prices outside the ETS often exceed those inside. In addition, as discussed earlier in this chapter, fuels used to generate electricity are exempt from taxes on fuel inputs, which includes carbon taxes, in most countries.

Debate on carbon taxes does not always take account of the existence of excise taxes, presumably because of the different policy intentions behind both taxes (roughly, carbon abatement or revenue raising) or because of views that carbon taxation should be additional to any existing taxes. Furthermore, the ways revenues are used also differs between the two instruments. Carbon tax revenues are often earmarked (e.g. for green spending), while excise tax revenue mostly flows into the general budget. When it is earmarked, this tends to go to spending on infrastructure, on the basis of the benefit principle.

Different policy rationales and design principles can result in differences in the salience of taxes. For example, there is some evidence that carbon taxes trigger larger demand responses than excise taxes or market price fluctuations. For example, David and Kilian (2011), Rivers and Schaufele (2016) and Andersson (2017) find that increases in carbon or energy taxes are more salient than equivalent changes in market prices. This is partly due to the political visibility of a tax introduction or rate increase and the expected longevity of the price signal compared to market price changes.

There is less evidence on differences between carbon and energy tax changes, but Rivers and Schaufele (2015) argue that carbon tax changes could be more salient than other excise taxes due to the explicit appeal to accelerate environmentally-friendly behaviour. In practice, the distinction between carbon and excise taxes might not be so sharp. Carbon taxes are usually translated from a rate per tonne of carbon to a rate in per unit of energy (e.g. litres or tonnes), so energy users, over the longer run, may only perceive the sum of carbon tax and excise tax rates.

Figure 2.22. **Proportion of CO_2 emissions from energy use subject to different levels of effective tax rates from carbon taxes in countries with a carbon tax**
(biomass emissions included)

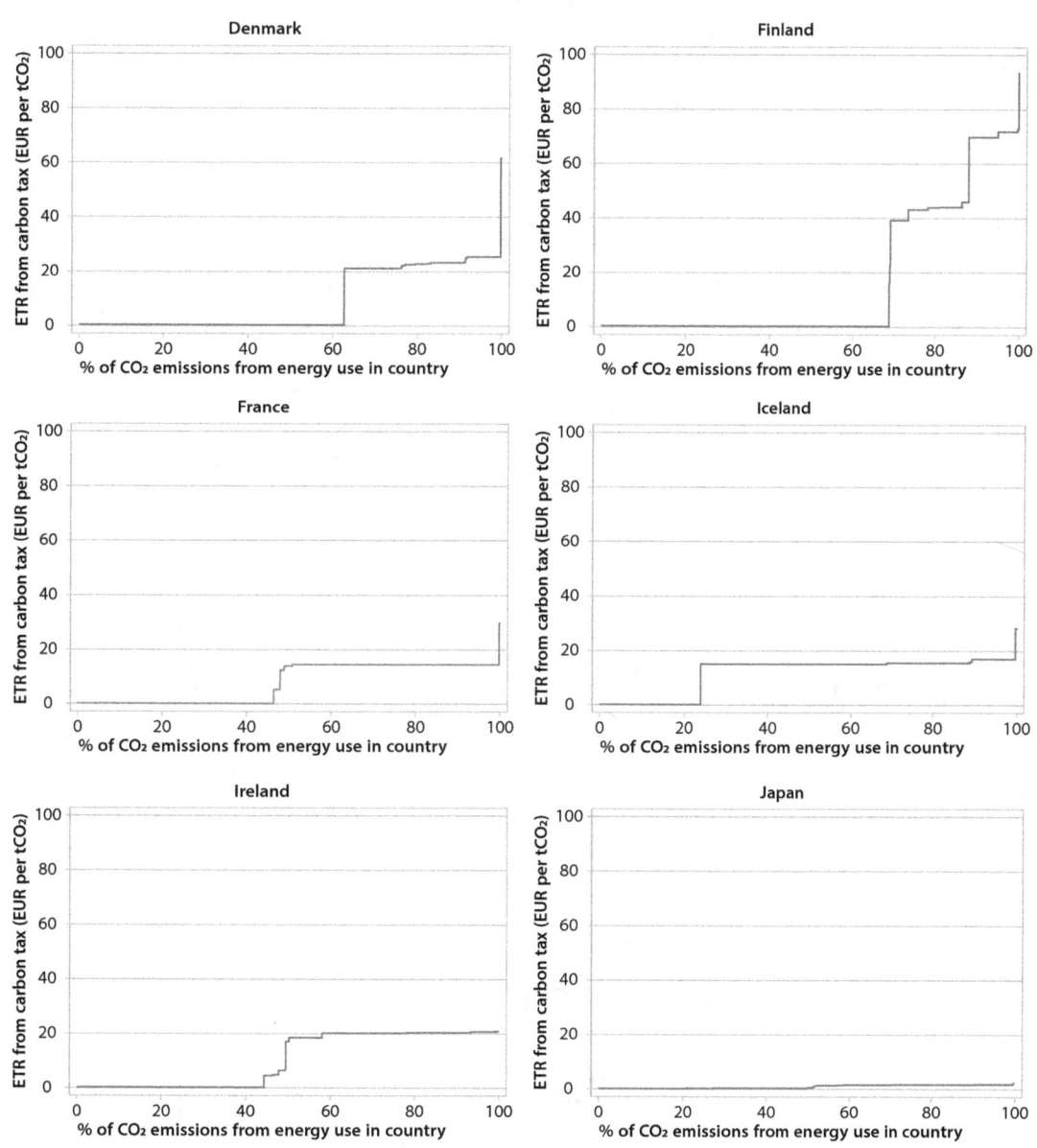

Figure 2.22. **Proportion of CO_2 emissions from energy use subject to different levels of effective tax rates from carbon taxes in countries with a carbon tax (biomass emissions included)** *(continued)*

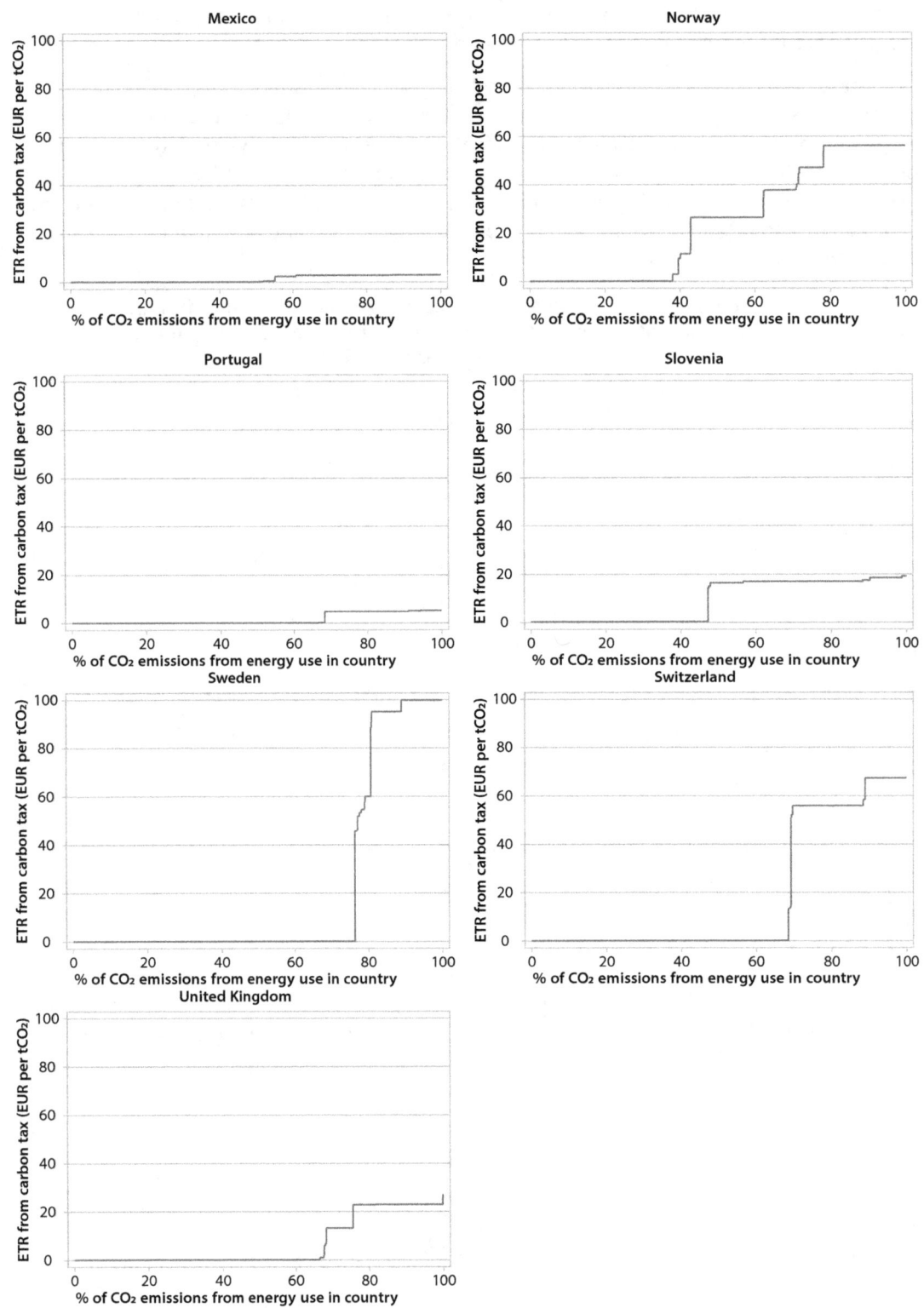

Note: All carbon tax rates are shown as at 1 April 2015. Carbon emissions from energy use were calculated from data in the *Extended World Energy Balances* (IEA, 2016b).

Conclusion

This report has discussed patterns of taxes on energy use by sector and by fuel, in 42 countries representing 80% of world energy use and of the CO_2 emissions from energy use, considering taxes in 2015 and changes from 2012 to 2015. The discussion finds that these taxes, with few exceptions, are poorly designed from an environmental and revenue-raising point of view. Changes in the patterns from 2012 to 2015 show some modest improvement of alignment with external costs, mainly as a result of road fuel tax increases in emerging economies.

Apart from some modest steps forward in a couple of countries, there is little evidence of better use of taxes on energy use to address the mounting global environmental and climate challenges. Instead, real tax rates are gradually eroded by inflation in most countries, suggesting indifference to the environmental efficacy of taxes. Evidence on emissions trading systems, not covered in this report but in OECD (2016), does little to change this rather bleak picture. Similarly, debate on carbon taxation is intense, and this debate has translated into action to a limited degree, however, such action remains insufficient to drive any meaningful changes to the actual tax rates.

Political economy considerations related to competitiveness and equity among households are partly responsible for the patterns observed, along with the influence on policy outcomes of sectional and interest groups. While these considerations are sometimes justifiable, there can be little doubt that their presence as a barrier to reform remains pervasive and real. A key policy recommendation from this work is that providing compensation for the cost increases from energy taxes, where deemed necessary, should not be provided through reduced rates or exemptions, but instead through targeted transfers that maintain the environmental integrity of market-based instruments.

References

Andersson, J. (2017), "Cars, carbon taxes and CO_2 emissions", Grantham Research Institute on Climate Change and the Environment, Working Paper No. 212.

Arlinghaus, J. and K. Van Dender (2017), "The environmental tax and subsidy reform in Mexico", *OECD Taxation Working Papers*, No. 31, OECD Publishing, Paris, http://dx.doi.org/10.1787/a9204f40-en.

Bureau of Transportation Statistics (2015), "Diesel-powered passenger cars and light trucks", https://www.rita.dot.gov/bts/sites/rita.dot.gov.bts/files/publications/bts_fact_sheets/oct_2015/html/entire.html (accessed 20 November 2017).

Davis, L.W. and L. Kilian (2011), "Estimating the Effect of a Gasoline Tax on Carbon Emissions." *Journal of Applied Econometrics*, 26: 1187-1214.

Enerdata (2018), "Rise in global energy-related CO_2 emissions in 2017", https://www.enerdata.net/publications/executive-briefing/global-increase-co2-emissions-2017.html.

Groothuis, F. (2016), *New era. New plan. Europe. A fiscal strategy for an inclusive, circular economy*, The Ex'tax Project Foundation, Utrecht, 2016.

Harding, M. (2014), "The Diesel Differential: Differences in the Tax Treatment of Gasoline and Diesel for Road Use", *OECD Taxation Working Papers*, No. 21, OECD Publishing, Paris, http://dx.doi.org/10.1787/5jz14cd7hk6b-en.

IEA (2016a), *World Energy Balances* (database), www.iea.org/statistics/topics/energybalances.

IEA (2016b), *Extended World Energy Balances* (database), www.iea.org/statistics/topics/energybalances.

IEA (2016c), *Medium-Term Coal Market Report 2016*, IEA, Paris, http://dx.doi.org/10.1787/mtrcoal-2016-en.

Mahler, A. et al. (2017), *Die Finanzierung Deutschlands über Steuern auf Arbeit, Kapital und Umweltverschmutzung* [Financing Germany via taxes on labour, capital and pollution], Forum Ökologisch Soziale Marktwirtschaft e.V./Green Budget Germany, www.foes.de/pdf/2017-06-Hintergrundpapier-Steuerstruktur.pdf.

OECD (2017), *Environmental Fiscal Reform: Progress, Prospects and Pitfalls, OECD Report for the G7 Environment Ministers*, https://www.oecd.org/tax/tax-policy/environmental-fiscal-reform-G7-environment-ministerial-meeting-june-2017.pdf.

OECD (2016), *Effective Carbon Rates: Pricing CO_2 through Taxes and Emissions Trading Systems*, OECD Publishing, Paris, http://dx.doi.org/10.1787/9789264260115-en.

Rivers, N. and B. Schaufele (2015), "Salience of carbon taxes in the gasoline market", *Journal of Environmental Economics and Management*, Volume 74, November 2015, p. 23-26.

Santos, G., (2017), "Road fuel taxes in Europe: do they internalize road transport externalities?" *Transport Policy*, 53, 120-134.

Van Dender, K. (2018, forthcoming), "Taxing vehicles, fuel, and road use: what mix for road transport?" OECD Taxation Working Paper.

World Bank (2017), *World Development Indicators 2017*, Washington, DC, World Bank, https://openknowledge.worldbank.org/handle/10986/26447.

Notes

1. As in the remainder of this document, effective tax rates on biofuels are shown separately, also to accommodate for different views on accounting for the carbon emissions from biofuels.

2. The Clean Coal Cess was since renamed to Clean Environment Cess, and currently applies at a rate of INR 400 to all coal, lignite and peat use.

3. Mahler et al. (2017) analyse the consequences of not adjusting nominal energy tax rates for inflation in Germany. They find that if energy tax rates would have been adjusted for inflation between 2004 (with 2003 being the last year in which energy tax rates were increased) and 2017, revenues would have been almost EUR 80 bln higher over the entire period (measured in 2017 prices). For example, had the energy tax on gasoline been adjusted for inflation between 2004 and 2017, it would be at EUR 0.78 per litre today, instead of the current EUR 0.6545 per litre, an increase of almost 20%.

4. The OECD has (tentatively) translated New Zealand's RUCs into a fuel tax equivalent, taking account of drivers' expected differential response to distance-based charges compared to fuel taxes (calculations are not shown here). The results suggest that if the RUCs were included into the TEU database as a fuel tax equivalent, the gap between the tax rates on diesel and gasoline would be narrower, but would remain substantial.

5. The relationships are similar between road and non-road sectors, so the graphs are not shown separately.

6. Note that several Canadian provinces levy specific taxes on carbon, but since they apply at subnational level they are not included in the *Taxing Energy Use* database.

ORGANISATION FOR ECONOMIC CO-OPERATION AND DEVELOPMENT

The OECD is a unique forum where governments work together to address the economic, social and environmental challenges of globalisation. The OECD is also at the forefront of efforts to understand and to help governments respond to new developments and concerns, such as corporate governance, the information economy and the challenges of an ageing population. The Organisation provides a setting where governments can compare policy experiences, seek answers to common problems, identify good practice and work to co-ordinate domestic and international policies.

The OECD member countries are: Australia, Austria, Belgium, Canada, Chile, the Czech Republic, Denmark, Estonia, Finland, France, Germany, Greece, Hungary, Iceland, Ireland, Israel, Italy, Japan, Korea, Latvia, Luxembourg, Mexico, the Netherlands, New Zealand, Norway, Poland, Portugal, the Slovak Republic, Slovenia, Spain, Sweden, Switzerland, Turkey, the United Kingdom and the United States. The European Union takes part in the work of the OECD.

OECD Publishing disseminates widely the results of the Organisation's statistics gathering and research on economic, social and environmental issues, as well as the conventions, guidelines and standards agreed by its members.

OECD PUBLISHING, 2, rue André-Pascal, 75775 PARIS CEDEX 16
(23 2018 04 1 P) ISBN 978-92-64-28943-7 – 2018